A Space for Soul

Nancy J. Lankston

Moonbeam Books
Colorado

A SPACE FOR SOUL

Copyright © 2014 Nancy J. Lankston

Library of Congress Control Number: 2014907482

Moonbeam Books, Boulder, Colorado

ISBN-13: 978-0692200858
ISBN-10: 0692200851

for Eve
who never told her story

Also by Nancy J. Lankston:

A Still Place; One Woman's Journey Home

Contents

Preface

The reflections I share in this book come from personal journals I kept over the last 20 years; they are my notes from the trail. Writing is one tool I pull out and use all the time. Writing helps me cut through the brambles and confusion and find my way. This book is filled with helpful hints and hard won wisdom; things I want to remember as I continue on my journey.

I began my healing path as an ICU nurse. Today I teach and write about nature based healing, transformation and expanding consciousness. My work today is truly light years from where I began 20+ years ago.

Transforming from a "normal" nurse into a teacher of spiritual and shamanic techniques has not always been easy; it has involved peeling away layer after layer of who I was supposed to be, who I was taught to be, in order to connect with the real me. And I have often felt huge fear as I pushed myself to venture into new territory.

If this were a "normal" book about healing I would use these pages to describe the healing methods I have personally used. Then I would guide you in how to use those methods to heal yourself. But every person's healing is unique. My healing methods may not work for you. Ultimately, all healing involves learning to trust yourself and chart your own course.

My personal healing has been about learning how to open up to life and share my soul with the world. Often, this soul baring process has left me feeling like I am completely alone, blazing a new trail through a confusing and harsh wilderness; at those times I try to breathe, focus on the ground right in front of me and trust my soul's guidance as I inch my way along, one step at a time.

That feeling of being alone, out in the wilderness is why this book exists; I want you to realize that you are not alone. I am right there with you in spirit, applauding your efforts and encouraging you to keep going. I hope that by sharing these words with you, I can help you find your way home a little quicker.

Just Start

Every season has a sound, and a different feel in the air.

Winter feels like deep, troubled sleep; tossing and turning, looking for quiet repose. It is the sound of the relentless north wind blowing through the trees. Then spring arrives feeling frenetic, busy - as though there is not nearly enough time to get everything done. The "hello, look at me" bird songs that fill the treetops, tell me spring has really arrived.

Summer is sleepy and abundant with the drone of cicadas rising and falling in the still hot afternoon air. In summer, the Earth seems to rest joyfully in her aliveness. Autumn comes and I feel a slowing of the pulse as the growing cycle slows down to a whisper.

As I write this, autumn is here. I can hear it. I lie in bed and listen to the nighttime sounds of the autumn woods; a cricket suddenly playing a violin solo in the silence; a solitary tree frog tentatively adds to the melody. The wind whispers through the leaves overhead. It's all Zen music for my soul.

In the morning, there is mist filling the valley behind the house. For the second time this week, I look out of my kitchen window to discover that the pond no longer exists at the bottom of the hill. The waters have been swallowed up in a silvery shroud of fog that hugs the hillside.

Not a breath of wind stirs and the mist feels sharp and cool in my throat, just as autumn air should feel. I can see my own breath ebb and flow as I stand on the deck straining to catch a glimpse of the pond below. As I peer out into the clouds, my busy schedule recedes and fades away. Life becomes still and utterly serene for a brief time. It is a tiny slice of peace in the midst of my morning chaos.

The geese that live in the pond appear to be struggling with a chaos of their own making. I can hear them honking and flying in circles around the pond and yard. They are disturbed, excited - something

1

is up. Is it time to fly south? Are southern waters calling to them? I do not hear the call, but I can sense their frenzy as they circle.

It must be scary for the young geese to feel the urge to leave and not know where they will end up… kind of like writing.

I begin this journey not knowing exactly what lies ahead. Any act of traveling into new uncharted territories, whether by wing or by pen, must be powered by faith. I tell myself to just take a deep breath and start.

Just start. Take it one stroke at a time…

Be Still

Why are you so enchanted by this world,
when a mine of gold lies within you?

~Rumi

Treasure Within

The outer world is so loud
and filled with self-importance.

Yet, the secret places hidden
Deep inside
Hold vast treasure.

Pause and listen within
Make space for stillness
Wisdom will surface.

Bathtub Diving

I remember `diving' in the bathtub as a child. Holding my breath until it felt as though my chest would explode and splinter into a million pieces, I wanted to stay underwater longer and longer... forever if I could.

When I got older, I loved diving in the lake near my house. I loved the shadowy green liquid world that muffled sound and touched me so tenderly as I slid through it. And I loved lake water the best; murky green with yellow bars of light slanting down into the depths.

I used to dream of being a fish, able to stay in liquid state forever. What a miracle it would be to have gills! It was the underwater light and utter stillness that drew me.

The same stillness draws me to meditation. As I sit in the silence, it feels as though my soul is surrounded by shadowy green wetness. I am enfolded and caressed as I glide into the depths. Only now it is the depths of myself that I seek, not a muddy lake bottom. I need no gills - just an open heart and a few moments in the silence.

In the shadowed stillness
I am at peace.
I glide into myself,
a sigh escapes.

Stillness

As I take a walk on a lake trail near my home, a huge thunderstorm is brewing just over the edge of the horizon. Thunder rumbles on the ridge, yet the lake water is still, perfectly still. Reflections of the foothills play on the surface of the water. The air is charged with magic potential.

I stare at the lake and my mind stills. And I remember a passage from one of my favorite books:

> *"The silence is all there is. It is the alpha and the omega.*
> *It is God's brooding over the face of the waters;*
> *it is the blended note of the ten thousand things,*
> *the whine of wings."*
>
> *~Annie Dillard, Teaching a Stone to Talk*

In the stillness before the storm, this space is alive with joy. Mother Nature shares her wisdom, whenever I remember to pause and listen.

Sitting

I sit with myself
I sit, I breathe
I scrawl words on paper
I feel happy and peaceful
I sit, I breathe
It begins to snow outside.
I sit, I breathe
I write word after word
I feel sad, so sad
an old wound exposed.

Snow falls.
I sit, I breathe
Machinery hums
outside, out of sight
but still with me
I sit, I breathe
My hip aches
my nose is numb
I sit, I breathe
and wonder, why numb?

The pitch of a roof outside
catches my gaze
I sit, I breathe
My hip aches
I breathe with the ache
the hum, the roof
Snow falls
I sit, I breathe
I feel hungry
the hum, the ache
and the roof go on.

In Praise of Solitude

*"Stop and listen to the heart, the wind outside, to one another,
to the changing patterns of this mysterious life. "*

~Jack Kornfield

For years I filled my life with constant noise. The TV or radio was my constant companion. Silence felt like an empty space that I needed to fill. There was never time in my day for a moment or two of quiet reflection. Then one day I "woke up" and looked around. I realized that I was miserable. I was only thirty-one, with a husband and a very successful career. Yet I felt horribly discontent and I had no idea why.

I went to church with a friend. I had not been to church since I was a teenager – I didn't like church. But this church that my friend took me to was different. This church had a ten-minute silent time in the middle of the service. I sat in the silence at that church, surrounded by strangers and I felt peace wash over me. I was more calm and content with myself than I had been in years. It was a revelation. After that one experience, I began searching for ways to put silence back into my life.

*"Perhaps it would be a good idea some day, fantastic as it
sounds, to muffle every telephone, quiet every motor, and stop
all activity – just to give people a chance to ponder and reflect
on what life is about, why they are living,
and what they really want."*

~James Truslow

Today, many years later, I still search for quiet and solitude. I close the door, turnoff the TV and just sit enjoying the quiet. Now that I have kids, one of my favorite tricks is to go lie in the bathtub with the water up over my ears. I can't hear the kids yelling when I have water in my ears! Wherever I go to be in the silence, my goal is simple: Do Nothing. Just breathe and BE with me for a few minutes.

"Far from being an indulgence, quiet, solitary contemplation -
"doing nothing" - is as restorative as any elixir."

~Stephan Rechtschaffen, M.D.

At times it seems impossible for me to get a few minutes alone in a quiet space –especially during the holiday season. Every spare moment is filled with holiday shopping, parties and noise and busyness. But on the days when I do find time to be still, I am so much more content. Alone time gets me recharged and focused and back in touch with myself.

Winter is the perfect season to cultivate a habit of quiet time. This is the season when Mother Earth gets quiet and still. Mother Earth knows that a season of quiet waiting in the dark is necessary to prepare for new growth.

"If one sets time aside for a business appointment or a social
engagement, that time is accepted as inviolable. But if anyone
says, "I cannot come because that is my hour to be alone," one
is considered rude, egotistical, or strange. What a sad
commentary on our civilization."

~Anne Morrow Lindbergh

The Little Voice Inside

When I started to "wake up" in my thirties and actively search for the meaning of life, I began attending church again. The church that I was drawn to was progressive. The minister pulled from many sources for her talks, weaving Buddhist sutras, Sufi quotes and even Jewish stories into her "Christian" message. Her eclectic mix felt fine. Underneath, all Gods are one and the same to me. I felt like I had found a spiritual home.

But one thing puzzled me. The minister would speak of getting guidance from God. She talked of having a little voice inside that gave her direction and pointed out her spiritual path to her. And she seemed certain that I had one too. For years I puzzled over this idea of divine guidance from within. I had always thought that realm was only open to priests, saints and mystics.

Oh, I had plenty of internal guidance. Some days my head positively buzzed with guidance. The problem was that I had more than one little voice inside me – I had several little voices with very distinct personalities and differing views on what exactly I should do with my day, week, and even my life! So, I puzzled over exactly which little voice was the voice of divine spirit guiding me and which was just the seductive pull of my ego in one of its many disguises.

After years of puzzling and wondering, I began to sense a pattern. I did have one little voice that was different from the others. It was a very quiet little voice, actually just a whisper. It was easily lost in the din of my thoughts. This voice was quiet and gentle yet very persistent. I began calling it "my little voice". And I noticed that when I listened and followed the guidance of this voice, life seemed to unfold in a very easy and organic way. Events would happen in synchrony – I would meet people who would have exactly what I needed when I needed it. And tiny miracles became a daily event; seemingly impossible problems would magically dissolve.

Life becomes a miraculous adventure
when I hear and heed my little voice.

The problem was (and still is) that I don't always pause and listen to my little voice. Sometimes I am too busy and my life gets too noisy. I absolutely require calm time in silence or my little voice gets lost in the din. And other times I hear my little voice, but I ignore it because what it is telling me seems too difficult or too scary. It may tell me to face a person or situation that is emotionally painful and I don't feel ready, willing or able to do that.

So, I experience serendipitous magical days when I listen to and follow the counsel of my little voice. And then there are the other days when I can't or won't hear. I suspect my life will continue to be about that dance, sometimes opening in love to God's plan and other times closing down and running away in fear. I think that's called being human.

But even when I close down in fear, my little voice continues to be quietly present. I am never alone. It is constant and unwavering. The tone of my little voice is never angry or upset, but rather calm and gentle. And she seems to always love me, no matter what I think, do or say. The advice she gives me is consistently kind – no one is ever harmed when I follow my little voice's counsel.

Sometimes I wonder what or who my little voice actually is. Is it my intuition? Divine Spirit? Christ? An angel? Is she giving voice to the great collective unconscious that Carl Jung spoke of? I suspect that it is somehow one and all of these at once.

In the end, what difference does it make what name I give the little voice inside me? I could call her Zeus if I wanted – just as long as I take time to pause and listen to her wisdom.

When I stop and listen to my little voice,
my life finds its own rhythm.

13

Pay Attention

"Life always gives us exactly the teacher we need at every moment. This includes every mosquito,every misfortune,every red light,every traffic jam,every obnoxious supervisor (or employee),every illness, every loss,every moment of joy or depression,every addiction, every piece of garbage,every breath.

Every moment is the guru.*"*

~Charlotte Joko Beck

The Art of Paying Attention

paying attention is simple

paying attention is much harder than it seems

paying attention is a form of prayer

paying attention is healing

paying attention is a radical act

in today's world

Wake Up

My experience of waking up: I take Dog Goddess Brigit on a walk by the river. We walk the same path almost every morning. And on many occasions, I have returned from our walk and realized that I didn't really notice my surroundings at all that day. I have been completely lost in my thoughts, unaware of what was right in front of me. I have been wrapped up in planning my future or ruminating on my past and the river slipped by unnoticed by me.

But some days are different; some days I actually focus on the path and my steps and the sounds on the wind. I notice the feel of the leash in my hand, the smell of some bush or tree nearby. And those moments when I am actually present and aware are so potent! On my *awake and aware* days, I notice many new things that I never noticed before – even though it is the exact same path Brigit and I walked yesterday.

An aware walk is magical.

It is as though I am more *alive* in aware moments. Waking up amps up my sensations and makes everything richer and fuller. For me, even being aware of something heavy and hard like sorrow or pain beats feeling half alive. I have learned that numbing out and avoiding yucky emotions and sensations comes at a price – if I numb out, I will also lose the yummy sensations and emotions that make my life sing.

Jon Kabat-Zinn describes awareness as being mindful, being present with whatever is in this moment. He calls it the art of "falling awake". Ram Das tells us to Be Here Now. Thich Nhat Hanh speaks of dwelling in the present moment. Not just living… *dwelling in the moment*. Seems like a very simple idea. And yet, I find it very difficult to pull off most days!

Modern life seems to be about distraction rather than awareness; we distract ourselves by turning on TV shows we only half watch. We woof down food we don't really even taste. We walk around dreaming of tomorrow or lamenting yesterday. We surf on the Internet, popping from screen to screen without really taking any of it in. We pride ourselves on being able to do 3 things at once, even when we can't actually remember much about doing any of them! Is that living?

I suspect that Dog Goddess Brigit is at least 100 times more aware than I am on any given day. My big, "superior" human brain gives me the ability to analyze and plan far beyond anything a dog can plan. And those same human abilities complicate the simple act of staying present and aware in this moment. My strength is also my weakness. Can I stop planning and analyzing long enough to notice what is here, right in front of me?

When it comes to being aware,
analysis is as useless as a dog chasing her own tail.

I wonder how much I miss when I am walking through my day half aware of what's around me here and now? What would it take for me to double or triple how many moments of the day that I am actually present?

What if I stop analyzing EVERYTHING and put my big, silly human brain to work sensing and perceiving what is here in front of me? What is the value of analyzing what happened yesterday if I miss today?

How much richer can my day-to-day reality become
if I make awareness my priority?

Beauty Here, Now

Pause and Breathe,

STOP doing,

BE HERE NOW!

There is beauty,

So much beauty

In the simplest of things.

Focus

A typical evening at my house; I try to write while my daughter plays music at high volume in the next room. Every few minutes, she runs into my office to show me something she's found on YouTube (any excuse to get mom's attention). The phone rings – my husband is on his way home. Uh oh, that means he is 15 minutes away and dinner is not quite done! I leap up from my desk to go into the kitchen and finish it. But my mind is still on my writing and I soon find myself frozen in mid-kitchen, trying to remember exactly why the refrigerator is open and what I am doing to dinner.

I have spent a HUGE portion of my adult life jumping from task to task like this, trying to get one task done while I am thinking about the next task… and the next… and the next. Constantly doing, constantly in motion – isn't it the American way?

My brain tends to jump from task to task naturally – is that the price of being a mom? Or maybe it's just "monkey mind". That's the term meditation instructors use to describe a mind that constantly in motion, constantly grasping at one thought and then the next. I have a bad case of monkey mind. I learned to meditate 20+ years ago in self-defense. Meditation is the only way I can get my mind to calm down and shut up for awhile!

All that jumping from thought to thought and task to task is really just a form of chasing my own tail. Back eons ago when I was a computer analyst, we called it "thrashing". Thrashing is what a computer does when it gets overloaded with work, The computer uses up all of its energy and time just pulling programs into working memory and then pushing them back out before anything can be accomplished. In severe cases of thrashing, no work gets done at all; but the poor computer keeps plugging away, working tirelessly to get it all done and actually accomplishing nothing.

Sounds like my ping ponging mind on a bad day.

But when I remember to slow down and focus on the one thing I am doing RIGHT NOW, to stop pushing to move on to the next task, then my life is so much calmer – and more enjoyable. AND I actually get more done.

After years of practicing meditation, I have come to believe that what I focus on in every moment is my choice. Life is coming at me faster and faster all the time. Technology makes it possible to attempt to do 3-4 things at once! I was thrilled to hear that the state where I live has outlawed texting while driving. Now maybe I won't kill myself trying to drive, text and adjust the radio simultaneously!

I can get sucked into racing around like an Indy 500 car, and end up thrashing; feeling like a victim of my hectic schedule and all the people that want something from me. But am I really a victim or am I making myself miserable?? I love what Eckhart Tolle wrote:

"True freedom is living as if you had completely chosen whatever you feel or experience in this moment. This inner alignment with the Now is the end of suffering."

Hmmm, maybe I actually get to decide for myself whether I suffer or I am joyful in every single moment of every single day. That is DEFINITELY NOT a modern American idea. If something goes wrong in the U.S., our first urge is to figure out who is to blame and then string them up in the press!

Blame seems to be more important than fixing the problem. An oilrig spews oil in the Gulf of Mexico and we decide that the CEO of British Petroleum is to blame. No, maybe the environmentalists are to blame – it's all those pesky drilling regulations! No wait – President Obama is to blame! SOMEBODY MUST PAY!

I am afraid that we're turning into a nation of finger pointing victims. Not Good.

In his book, *Present Moment, Wonderful Moment,* Zen master Thich Nhat Hanh offers this:

> *"Our mind is like a television with thousands of channels, and*
> *the channel we switch on is the channel we are at that*
> *moment. When we turn on anger, we are anger.*
> *When we turn on peace and joy, we are peace and joy.*
> *We have the ability to select the channel.*
> *We are what we choose to be."*

I don't know about you, but I want to 'change my channel' and stop racing through life so fast that I don't even notice where I am at or what I am doing. I want to choose to slow down and enjoy my life right now. And I want to pause, take a deep breath and stop blaming others.

This is MY life and MY thoughts and MY feelings. I can "change my channel" and take responsibility for every bit of my life. And I can have a wonderful, joyful calm day no matter what kind of craziness comes at me

Every Day is Sacred

Hours of forgetting
then a flash of sunlight
wind ruffles wet flesh

awash in sensation
heart stills, time stops
and I open myself
to this

falling awake
to sun and bone
wind on water

I am here
all here in
sacred space.

I Will Be Happy When...

Winter is not my favorite time of year. In fact, it is my least favorite. Winter in my neck of the woods seems to be filled with cold and gray days. February may be the shortest month, but it seems terminally long to me. I cannot wait until spring arrives with the smell of growth in the air.

Oops. I have fallen into my "I will be happy when..." trap again. I find myself focused on everything wrong with my day and fantasizing about being content when I have no more problems in the future. I will be happy when spring comes – I hate these cold, gray winter days. I will be happy when everyone is home tonight for dinner and my family can be together. I will be happy when I finish my book. I will be happy when I have a good hair day. I will be happy when I have more students. I will be happy when the sun shines. I will be happy when I solve that problem. I will be happy when...

Thinking this way means that my happiness never quite arrives. It is always just out there, a little ways in front of me. I can see it, smell it, almost taste it – but no, I CANNOT feel it until some point off in the future when all of the pieces of my life fall into perfect alignment and everything becomes heavenly. I put happiness out there, outside of me. If only other people and weather and circumstances would behave and do exactly what I want, THEN I could be content.

But my life is ticking away while I postpone happiness again and again. And all that wanting and needing and wishing for something to be different has NOTHING to do with true happiness. I have discovered that all it takes to feel more joy and contentment in my life is a shift in my attention.

If I can let go of past mistakes and future problems long enough to just be present right here and now, then joy and contentment come naturally to me. This little shift is called mindfulness.

In the introduction to *Present Moment, Wonderful Moment,* Thich Nhat Hanh describes mindfulness this way,

> *"When we settle into the present moment, we can see beauties and wonders right before our eyes – a newborn baby, the sun rising in the sky. We can be very happy just by being aware of what is in front of us."*

Thich Nhat Hanh is a Zen monk who lived through absolute horrors during the Viet Nam war. And instead of becoming jaded or bitter, he has spent the last 40 years teaching joyful, mindful living. His teachings appear very simplistic on the surface. Sometimes the simplest acts are the most difficult - and the most powerful.

Mindful awareness is a simple act – just focus on whatever I am doing right now. For example, when I wash the dishes, just focus on washing the dishes. When I drive, just focus on driving. When I listen to someone, just listen. And when my mind wanders, gently bring it back to the single task in front of me. Just BE present in this moment.

This wakeful way of living is a revelation to me. I have put conditions on my happiness for my entire life. But now I find that just by focusing on my breath and what is around me in this moment, I can shake my negative "if only this would happen..." loop. This one simple act helps me to feel unbelievably calm and content in the midst of a chaotic day.

So, I am working on – no, not working, that sounds too difficult. I am PRACTICING being mindful and noticing everything that is wonderful about the here and now. It is very hard at times. Like most Moms, I am trained to multi-task, to juggle three things at once. I am learning a new habit: one moment at a time.

Whenever I catch myself grousing about my lot in life and thinking "if only this would change, I would be happy" , I stop, take a deep breath and look closely at whatever is here in this present moment . I focus on just this moment in time and my mind clears. I find peace. It is like coming to ground after a long, deep meditation.

Right now in this moment, I take a deep breath and look around me. I pause and notice the warm glow I have in my belly as I write this.

I am content in this moment and I want to acknowledge my contentment. I want to notice what is peaceful and right about this moment.

What I focus on increases and I want more of this warm, peaceful, content feeling in every day. Yes, it is cold and gray outside and yes, my house is a complete mess and yes, my bank account is close to zero. BUT look how the bare tree branches appear to be etched into that gray sky – how incredibly gorgeous! And the cold weather brings the deer right up next to the house where I can watch them.

And best of all, I sit here doing one of the things that I love most in the world – writing.

Life is not so bad, after all.
In this moment I am happy.

Here and Now

Here and now it is sunny outside
I chop carrots. Mince garlic.
Heat oil. Salivate.
Inhale the aroma.

Here and now I am sad inside
I grieve. Shed tears
Ponder death.
See pain all around.

Here and now I sit with it all
Breathe pain. Breathe sorrow.
Breathe garlic and sun
Open to life.

Trust Spirit

"Have faith in the way things are"

~Lao Tzu, Tao Te Ching

To Be or Not To Be...
Do I really want to be conscious?

Time flies; I have been on this spiritual path for more than twenty years now. Funny, that sounds like I am talking about being in Narcotics Anonymous or "on the wagon". Actually, my spiritual path can feel a lot like drying out and going cold turkey at times. Some days, every single person I meet seems to have taken the Asshole Vow. It can be difficult to remember that I am still responsible for everything I do and say even when provoked by an asshole! On those days it can be very hard to want to stay awake and aware in the moment.

I know that what I put out in the world is what I get back. Call it the Golden Rule or Karma or the Boomerang Principle, whatever. That is how life works. But I must admit that sometimes I fantasize about the "good old days" before I discovered spirituality and meditation and yoga. The good old days when dealing with an asshole probably would have triggered a daylong rant on my part. I know that ranting won't keep a jerk from behaving badly. And blaming others always comes back to haunt me sooner or later. But sometimes spewing like a jerk right back at 'em would feel so delicious!

A few weeks ago after a long day when nothing seemed to go my way, I found myself lying in bed wide awake, fantasizing about being spiritually unconscious again. Oh, to be sleepwalking through my life again! How glorious to have my worst problem be something trivial like: how to pay for the latest electronic gadget, or how to shrink my wrinkles, or how to impress my neighbor by mowing my grass twice a week. That certainly sounds easier than working on quelling my childhood demons or seeking emotional peace.

Sometimes I just get tired of this endless
spiritual quest of mine.

On days when my life sucks swamp water and I turn on myself for my seemingly endless list of imperfections, I actually wish that I could flip a switch and go back to being spiritually unconscious. Go back to just getting up and going to a dull job and coming home and eating dinner before I go to bed and start the treadmill all over again. That life was simpler and I could always blame someone else for my problems and imperfections.

After more than 20 years of meditation and spiritual study and alternative therapy sessions designed to rid me of my inner demons and pain – after all this intense work on myself, I must admit that I am still not remotely close to becoming perfect. I still lose my temper. I still get bitchy and catty. I still gossip. I still procrastinate and avoid difficult tasks. And I still hide from people and things that scare me. So what is the deal here - am I walking backwards down this path or what??

I still have all the same personality flaws I had when I started my soul searching - only now I KNOW that I have no one to blame for my dysfunction except myself!

So, has this spiritual journey led me to a better place? Well, after all these years of self-awareness and self-improvement, I am now absolutely certain of one thing; I can be a real twit and I will continue to be a real twit off and on for the rest of my days. The bottom line is I will continue to mess up and misbehave and I will NEVER attain the perfection that I thought I was seeking when I started this journey.

But is life really meant to be all about pushing and striving until at some point in the future, I FINALLY get it all right and perfection is attained? Gandhi said that I must be the change I wish to see in the world. Did he mean that I should turn myself into an endless fix-it project?? Absolutely not!

My biggest spiritual lesson is to realize that my flawed imperfect self is OK – no, more than OK, I am EXACTLY as I should be. No improvement is required.

I don't need to turn into a perfect wife, mommy or therapist. Losing my temper is not the end of the world. My house can be filthy and I'm still lovable. And it's actually OK to be whiny and needy at times. I don't need to overflow with insight and healing in every single therapy session. And everything I write does not need to be profound.

Perfection is not required. It's a HUGE relief to realize that. To know that I am OK – no matter how messy my life is. The title of Thomas Harris' classic book summed it up: *I'm OK, You're OK*. I read that book over 30 years ago, and I am just beginning to understand its simple message.

Stay awake. Pay attention. Love and accept myself. That's my mission. And all I need is a willingness to wake up and notice what is really going on right in this moment. I need to be willing to see and accept myself just as I am, warts and all. And be willing to love myself no matter how messy I get.

Yes, I still want to change the world and make it a better place. I still want to help and serve others. But I now see that I cannot serve ANYONE effectively unless I first love and honor and serve myself. I have to start with me.

Can peace be as close as that? What a startling idea after all the years I tried to fix myself with spiritual practices! Loving myself just as I am is the answer. No matter what happens, open my heart in love for myself. So simple and so hard to do! But when I do accept myself as I am and open in love, then I feel true joy. Even a few moments of self-acceptance are truly blissful. And I find that if I accept and love myself, then loving and serving others begins to flow naturally from me.

My new mantra is I'm OK. I'm OK. I'm really OK!

On days when I can open my heart to myself and resonate with being OK, I feel a deep joy down to my bones. And I know that I have found the peace I set out to find 20+ years ago. One moment at a time, I can create a life that I want to stay awake for.

Finding Ground

"What is rooted is easy to nourish."

~Lao Tzu, Tao Te Ching

Yesterday the dogwood tree in my yard was covered with green leaves; this morning all but two low branches are deep maroon. Amazing how fast that shift happened. Autumn has been whispering its way towards my town for weeks. The wild rainstorm yesterday seems to have signaled its official arrival. The air is cooler, crisper today. And I notice leaves turning yellow, orange and maroon everywhere I look. Changes in my personal life are like that; little hints of change and subtle shifts happen that I often miss or ignore. Then, wham, a storm blows through, and in the aftermath I look around surprised to see profound changes in myself and in those around me.

I took a walk down the creek path this morning. The day is gorgeous; sunny with a cool wind and high wispy clouds in a bright blue sky. Jacket weather is here; quite a contrast with yesterday's cold gray skies and hours of torrential downpour. The heavy rains left the creek high, very high. And the storm water has noticeably altered the creek in just one day. In one spot, long hairy orange tree roots dangle in mid-air over the far curve of the creek bank. Yesterday the roots were encased in dirt; today they dangle free and unsupported. I have had days like that - I wake up to discover that the very ground I have been rooted in and attached to is suddenly gone.

Most humans are not very good at handling change and I am no exception. With change comes fear; that feeling of the world shifting out from under me, of dangling in mid-air without support is very scary. Sometimes I get stuck in that state of fear and I start to worry that problems and instability are all I have to look forward to.

I say that I believe in a benevolent God; a God who takes care of the earth and all living creatures; a God who it omnipotent and all knowing; a God from which all of life flows. And yet when my path gets rough or the world seems dark, I have trouble trusting that God truly does know what she is doing and all is well.

Any change or shift in my life can trigger the fear. The shift can be something as simple as a change in my schedule or diet, or as profound as divorcing my first husband. The size or importance of the shift does not necessarily determine how well I cope with the change. Any shift, big or small, can be difficult.

The trees on the creek bank seemed to handle change better than I normally do. Trees instinctually know to lean away from instability and sink new roots into whatever ground is left to support them. In contrast, I flounder for days, feeling angry and off balance, bemoaning whatever changed in my life. I grieve for the support I lost. I forget to breathe and lean into the support I still have.

Trees have a visceral trust in the Universe or earth to support them and provide for them no matter what happens. I have trouble trusting in the good of the Universe in the midst of change. I get caught up in grieving what I have lost instead of opening to what is now possible. I forget to pray or meditate and I lose my connection to ground.

Faith and trust in the good of God is my ground, the core bedrock that won't shift out from under me no matter what. For me, faith and trust come from cultivating my internal KNOWING sense of God as good and benevolent rather than mean or indifferent. That loving essence of God is always with me, around me, within me. I sense it when I work with clients, when I pray, when I watch children play, when I hug someone. And yet I also forget it again and again. I lose my connection to God and I flounder.

Buddhism tells me that I suffer when I cling and grasp, when I try to keep things from changing. Nothing is permanent except Buddha or God. And Christianity tells me to build my faith on the rock of Christ. Judaism implores me to trust in the Lord. Peace of mind comes from letting go and trusting that God or Buddha is in charge. Letting go and trusting in God to handle the affairs of the world is the only answer.

I find that I must tend to my trust and faith like a tender young seedling in my garden. My faith needs to soak up the sun of other people's loving, positive energy. And then I must water it with prayer and meditation; and trust that it already knows how to grow. I must feed my faith by actively noticing the good in people, the love in the world.

Water and feed, water and feed until my tiny bit of faith and trust in the good of God grows stronger, more resilient, more certain. Water and feed my seedling again and again until one day I discover that my seedling has grown bigger and stronger and is deeply rooted in all directions.

When I am anchored in faith, change no longer throws me into doubt and fear. I can be as calm as the trees on the bank of the creek. I can remember that all is well.

"All shall be well and all shall be well
and all manner of things shall be well."

~St. Julian of Norwich

On Faith and Forsythias

As I write this, I can hear the wind blowing and blowing around the eaves of the house. Spring is blowing into town.

The forsythia bushes are blooming - another sign that spring is really here. I love watching the way each forsythia bush changes from a nondescript tangle of bare branches into an outrageously yellow beacon of spring. It seems magical to me; a few weeks ago my forsythia looked like a lifeless pile of dead branches, a lost cause. And now every branch is covered with tiny yellow stars winking at me.

Forsythia bushes seem to bloom just when I fear that the winter will never end. After days and days of cloudy, dreary weather, one day I look up and the sun is shining and the forsythia bushes seem to be shouting with joy, saying "Look! It's spring!"

Forsythia bushes are God's way of reminding me to have faith and not give up hope. New growth is always possible no matter how cold and gloomy the world appears to be.

I have never seen a forsythia bush get fooled by false spring weather in February and bloom early. How do they do that? How do they know when to wait and when to bloom? Some inner clock, I suppose. My own life certainly goes much smoother if I know when to wait and when to act. That inner knowing seems to flow naturally within me if I live mindfully

When the forsythia decides to bloom, I get the itch to garden. Spring means it is time to get down and dig my fingers into the earth, to feel and smell the change of seasons. Mother earth smells vibrant and alive beneath my fingernails in the spring. The smell of spring soil is a healing elixir for my soul.

Gardening is all about faith; I plant seeds in the ground, water them and then wait. And then wait some more.

After a week or two of waiting and watching, I finally spy the first tiny sprouts of life poking out of the earth. Soon an entire plant is growing where there was once bare earth. Once again, Mother Nature offers me a basic lesson in faith.

"None of us knows what might happen
even the next minute, yet still we go forward.
Because we trust. Because we have Faith."

~Paul Coelho

Seeds of Possibility

I take an early morning walk; it is already promising to be a hot day. But here by the river, it is still cool and juicy and green. The dog and I wander down the river trail, and I begin to see seeds everywhere... Seeds dangle above me, below me, in front of me. Seeds on grass stalks, trees ripe with seed, every weed flowering and throwing off seeds in the wind. Every plant seems to be going to seed right before my eyes.

Seeds symbolize potential for me; each seed is a tiny, little pocket of possibility. From a biological perspective, seeds actually hold the blueprint for all of creation on planet earth. EVERY bit of life here starts with seed; seeds are the source of all the plants in the ocean and on land. And every animal on earth, including you and me, began from a tiny fertilized ovum seed.

Even after decades of gardening, I am still astounded each time I see life sprouting from a seed; I plant tiny black seeds the size of pepper grains in my garden, and within weeks, tiny seedlings sprout and transform into big heads of yummy green lettuce. Nature orchestrates a miraculous transformation from seed potential to juicy plant reality in just a few short weeks.

"The creation of a thousand forests is in one acorn."

~Ralph Waldo Emerson

One tiny plant seed, combined with a little water and sunlight, will grow into a cottonwood tree or a clump of grass. Or maybe even an entire meadow full of blooms. The creative possibilities from one seed are staggering. Every single little seed holds magical possibilities. And Mother Nature is obviously a gifted magician.

I walk by the river, spying seeds at every turn. It is as though nature is teasing and taunting me with the abundant possibilities of life.

The sight of seeds dangling from every tree, bush and grass stalk is so outrageously over the top that I cannot help but smile at all this abundance.

Seeds are just the message I need today; I have been working on a book about elemental flow for months, struggling to create a structure that will hold the ideas that want to burst forth onto paper. But this particular piece of writing is as slippery and elusive as an eel; it slithers away each time I think I've finally got it pinned down.

I have been trying to grab this elusive little book and hold it still so I can define it, but it defies all my efforts at solid definition. This particular book creation seems to thrive on chaos and confusion. And the final shape of this book is not remotely in sight yet. I find that I am a bit fearful of not having any sense of where this book and I are going to end up.

Like most writers and artists, I love to pretend that I am in control of my creative process – even when I know in my heart that I'm not! When I am honest with myself, I admit that my husband's view of my writing being some type of mysterious, organic secretion process is actually more accurate!

But here, on the river path this morning, I look around and see how Nature is absolutely pouring her creative juices into a future that can't yet be seen. Mother Nature doesn't sit and whine about not being able to predict the final shape of her creative efforts; she doesn't refuse to proceed with seed production until the future is defined and absolutely known. Mother Nature just creates… and keeps creating and creating. I believe she creates just for the sheer joy of creating.

"Nourish beginnings, let us nourish beginnings.
Not all things are blest, but the seeds of all things are blest.
The blessing is in the seed."

~Muriel Rukeyser

I look around at all of Mother Nature's creations and I remember that creativity is more about allowing than controlling. My attempts at control usually end up killing my creative flow. Creativity LOVES free and unconfined spaces.

My own writing moves into a magical space when I stop worrying about the final outcome, and just open up and allow the flow of ideas. Allow the flow of words to come out in whatever form they choose to take today. The final product will take care of itself if I can relax and breathe, and just follow today's flow. Relax and allow the words to flow without trying to clamp down and judge them or filter them or manipulate them.

I breathe in the sights and scents of Mother Nature's creative abundance. I breathe and feel myself relax. Like every seed on my path today, this elusive book knows what it wants to become, even if it won't reveal itself to me yet. My job is to allow it to flow out into the light of day and to water it with my loving attention.

Use What You're Given

"Every situation, no matter how challenging,
is conspiringto bring you home to you."

~Panache Desai

A nasty February blizzard is cooking outside – the wind is blowing so hard that the snow is not falling to the ground so much as blowing south horizontally. I watch it blow like stink and Thank God for indoor plumbing… I cannot imagine having to wade out to an outhouse in this!

So, what goes best with a blizzard? It's definitely den time with the family. And I find myself craving soup. Yes, soup sounds yummy. But I hadn't really planned on making soup this weekend. I didn't buy soup fixin's…

What to do, what to do? Hmmm, maybe I can use what I've been given and rustle up some soup anyway. I love a challenge. After rummaging through the refrigerator, here's what went into the soup this morning:

> 1/2 onion, chopped
> 1 celery stalk, chopped
> 1 cup fresh spinach leaves   I live on greens – my nickname around here is Popeye, so I always have spinach or kale or something green in the fridge.
> 1/2 roast chicken, bones removed, skin tossed in to make broth. I use leftover roast chicken from 5 nights ago. I bought it when I didn't feel like cooking.
> 1/2 lime, juiced   I've never put this in soup before, so it's purely experimental.
> 1 Clove garlic   Required – my hubby LOVES garlic in everything.
> Salt and Pepper to taste

In an hour I will pull out the chicken skin, add more water and toss in 1cup of rice and 1 tsp. dried lemongrass. Then I just let it simmer a few minutes longer. Even now, the smell is starting to fill the house and make my mouth water!

Use what you're given is something I learned from a little book called *Instructions to the Cook* by Glassman & Fields. These two Zen practitioners ran charities that provided food and housing for the homeless on a shoestring budget for years. And in the process, they became masters at creating something special from whatever they were given. Their little gem of a book inspires me to stop, take a deep breath and figure out a way to happily use whatever life is giving me in this moment.

Open Your Heart

"Love the world as your self;
then you can care for all things."

~Lao Tzu, Tao Te Ching

Open Wide

Advice to myself...

Open your heart to every experience,

and watch life become magical.

A closed heart is worse than death.

Only an open heart can truly receive.

Embrace all that Life offers.

Open wide.

Spacious Heart

*"The little space within the heart
is as great as the vast universe..."*

~Swami Prabhavananda

What happens if I stay open hearted and vulnerable, no matter what happens around me? Can I be spacious and hard-hearted? No, when my heart is open and spacious, my mean malicious thoughts just blow away.

Can I have a spacious heart and be sad? No, not for long – if I hold my heart open and allow my grief and sadness to flow, they wash away. Isn't that what Jesus and Gandhi and Buddha taught – to stay open hearted and spacious?

I am reminded of a story I read once about the Dalai Lama; a woman came to see the Dalai Lama and told him about how she and other Buddhist nuns had been put down, abused and mistreated by the male monks in their spiritual communities. Upon hearing her story, the Dalai Lama bowed his head and wept.

He wept openly in the middle of his great hall, surrounded by his advisors. He wept openly in front of the many important people who were waiting to speak to him. And everyone sitting in the great hall that day with the Dalai Lama was changed. They were changed because the Dalai Lama dared to embody vulnerability and a spacious heart for everyone to see and feel.

*I choose a spacious heart today.
I choose spacious even when it feels scary and exposed.
I choose spacious even when it takes my breath away.
I choose spacious.*

Smoke and Stone

I sit
breathing out my worry
and my wonder
as I silently ask the Goddess
what exactly is compassion?
And can I offer it to myself?

I sit
breathing out my fear
am I brave enough
to love like a Boddhisattva
without reason,
without end?

I sit
watching the Goddess
smoke dances, we sit
suddenly, the stone of me cracks
there is nowhere to hide
I am love.

Fading Away

My mom's name is Eve and she was born in 1925. My mom may have been born in 1925, but she really resonated with the feminist ideals of the 1960's. Even though her career was staying home and raising four kids, Mom instinctually understood the basic feminist message; women deserve to have a choice about how they live their lives. She understood that even as she allowed herself few of those same choices.

Mom may have been named after the first woman in the Bible, but the name Eve NEVER fit her. Mom never fit the mold of the good "little woman" who is made from her husband's rib and is subservient to her man and lives to serve him. No, my mom complained about the silly rules that dictate proper female behavior from the very beginning; as a kid, she demanded to know why her five brothers never had to do housework while she and her sister were cooking and cleaning up after them every week. And how come the boys got to swim in the creek, but she and her older sister couldn't? Apparently it wasn't proper in the 1930's for teenaged girls to swim in the creek, even when it was 95 degrees in the shade. Can you imagine?!

Later on as an adult, my mom wondered aloud why men got to do all different kinds of work while women were expected to marry and become homemakers. And she thought it very sad that an intelligent and beautiful woman like her sister who never married was labeled a spinster and considered broken by this society!

No, my mom was NEVER a mild mannered 'good little woman'. And I mean that as the highest compliment. Mom was actually more like Adam's first wife, Lilith. Most people have never heard of Adam's first wife Lilith, but she appears in the Jewish Talmud and several other sacred texts. Most references to Lilith were stripped from the Bible. And what, pray tell, was Lilith's crime? Well, Lilith refused to be subservient to Adam. She refused to "lie beneath him". And when Adam balked at treating her as his equal, Lilith up and left Adam and went to live by herself near the Red Sea.

For refusing to cleave to Adam and do what he said, Lilith was condemned by her culture and labeled an evil witch who ate newborn babies and sucked the virility right out of men. For "misbehaving" Lilith was rejected and labeled an uppity bitch. Sounds familiar, doesn't it? I picture a mix of a seductive Gloria Steinem and an angry Betty Friedan whenever I think of Lilith.

Lilith is the original feminist archetype; she's a powerful female who KNOWS she is complete unto herself and she needs no man to define her or validate her existence. Lilith resonates with that same powerful anger that drives modern feminists like myself; we feminists look around and see how women allow themselves to be treated and we roar with rage.

Unlike Lilith, my mom never left her husband. She never left, but she roared with rage at the inequities of her married life on many occasions. She roared but she really never figured out how to make her own marriage less traditional. It took me years to realize that Mom was actually raging at herself and her own decisions as much as anyone else.

I think Mom craved a small space of her own without the needs of a husband and four kids drowning out her own desires. Like millions of women before her, my mom craved a space of her own, but never figured out how to take it for herself.

When I asked my mom in her late 60's what she had dreamed of being when she was a girl, she had difficulty even answering me. She said she couldn't remember. Is it any wonder? 1920's society just assumed that girls would want to grow up and be a wife and mommy. So, give them dolls and teach them how to cook and clean, right? What a waste!

Mom must have felt such a conflict within herself for so long. She resonated with the feminist ideals of finding yourself and building a meaningful career, and yet she stayed in a traditional marriage and spent her days taking care of four kids and doing mind-numbing secretarial work.

Please don't get me wrong; my mom adored my dad. But she dreamed of something more than marriage for herself and for her daughters. She cajoled and encouraged and pushed me to take a different path; to be more than a wife and mommy, to graduate from college and find work that I could make my own. I have her to thank for this career that I love.

Even in her eighty's my mom was still feisty and opinionated. But after decades of denying any part of herself beyond wife and mommy, she developed Alzheimer's and slowly lost her mind. Is that just coincidence? I don't think so. Ironically as the disease progressed, Mom became less and less like feisty Lilith and more like docile Eve.

Mom died in November 2013, after suffering from Alzheimer's for over seven years.

As I write this, I remember watching my mom's brilliant wit and intelligence fade away, and I am sad. I am so sad for the loss of the outrageous woman who was my mother. And I am sad that my opinionated mother could not figure out how to hold onto herself and her opinions any longer. And I am very sad that my youngest daughter will never really know her grandmother's strength or her powerful presence.

I love you Mom. I miss you. Thanks for everything you taught me about being a woman. Safe travels. May your doors and gates and paths be open as you travel beyond this place.

Embrace It All

What would it take for me to embrace it ALL?

Growth AND decay

Wrong AND right

Clarity AND confusion

Dark AND light

Joy AND sorrow?

Life is messy.

What would it take for me to open my heart,

& receive EVERYTHING the world offers up to me?

The View From Here

I am pondering today: How much do my "views" about the world actually shape my future experiences in the world? How much do my beliefs about the world and how life works create the form my future takes? Do I usually get what I believe I will get?

This seems especially relevant to me in 2012 as the United States enters the home stretch of a particularly nasty and malicious presidential election. And this is also an election where the 2 main presidential candidates have *very* different viewpoints about the world and how it all "works." So, which viewpoint do I vote for? And does my vote even matter? How much might this one little choice alter my future?

Years ago, two amazing change agents named Jerry Weinberg and Jean McLendon introduced me to an eye-opening model of perception and reality:

Malicious, Stupid or Kind?

Do I see my world as **Mean and malicious**? Do I believe that people are out to hurt me and reject me? Do events seem to conspire against me? Do I live in fear that God is watching and waiting to punish me?

Or is my world **Stupid**? Does everyone I meet seem to be a moron? Do I believe that I am the only one that knows what's going on around here – is everyone else just too stupid to see the truth?

Or do I live in a **Kind** world? Are people basically caring and kind? Do people love me? Do they want to assist me and help me? Is God supporting me and helping me in every moment?

Note: this model was originally created by family therapist Virginia Satir. I LOVE this model! When I take the time to ponder it and use it, I realize just how much I sabotage myself by approaching the world like it is out to hurt me or trip me up and get in my way.

When I remember to ask myself just one simple question, I can shift right out of my "poor me story" about whatever is happening in my life that is bothering me:

Which Universe am I living in today?

Is life loving and kind today? Or is it mean and malicious? Asking which Universe I find myself in helps me stop whining and blaming others almost instantly. I am able pause and gain a bit of perspective. And when I ask this question a lot, I begin to see how I add to my own misery every time I approach the world from any space other than kindness and benevolence.

What happens when I assume a kind Universe, a benevolent God who is just waiting to lovingly help and support me? What happens to my day? And what would happen if I choose to make kindness my religion?

"My religion is very simple.
My religion is kindness."

~Dalai Lama

My heart opens whenever I read this quote from the Dalai Lama. And that's the energy I feel emanating from the Dalai Lama; pure kindness and love. I bet HE inhabits a kind and caring Universe most days.

So, here I sit pondering my personal life and global events... How much does my viewpoint matter? Do my little choices actually matter? And does being kind make any difference in the world?

I say YES! I choose to matter. And I choose kindness - because in my world, change happens one kind little choice at a time.

55

Seeing the World as Sacred

*"The way we see the world shapes the way we treat it.
If a mountain is a deity, not a pile of ore; if a river is one of the
veins of the land, not potential irrigation water; if a forest is a
sacred grove, not timber; if other species are biological kin, not
resources; or if the planet is our mother, not an opportunity –
then we will treat each other with greater respect. Thus is the
challenge, to look at the world from a different perspective."*

~David Suzuki

I climbed up Buffalo Ridge yesterday. I nicknamed this ridge
southeast of my home Buffalo Ridge months ago – the spot just has
the energy of buffalo roaming free for me. Well, yesterday I climbed
to the top of Buffalo Ridge. And now, as I stare out my window at
that ridge, it looks completely different to me. Maybe it's because I
have been talking about climbing this ridge for 2 years and I
FINALLY did it! Yes, that's definitely part of the shift.

But my internal shift involves more than just accomplishing
something that I set out to do; Buffalo Ridge is now known to me in
a completely different way. I have an intimate relationship with this
ridge now. I look out at Buffalo Ridge and see the rocks I scrambled
over to reach the very top. And I see the circle of old pines that I sat
beneath and rested. I remember startling the deer that were bedded
down on its slope in the heat of mid-day. And I can still see the
cactus on the verge of blooming as well as a thousand tiny white
wildflowers already in full bloom.

Today I look out the window and I don't just see a rocky ridge that I
climbed. I see a loving ally that watches over my home and
neighborhood. And I see a friend who shared her beautiful secrets
with me. I am connected to the ridge in a deeper way now.
Somehow, Buffalo Ridge opened my heart.

Let Go

*"We must be willing to let go of the life we've planned,
so as to have the life that is waiting for us."*

~Joseph Campbell

Relax and Allow

"Let go or be dragged."

~Zen Proverb

I am a very willful and opinionated person. And in many ways, my tendency to know and speak my own mind has been one of my strengths. No one has ever accused me of being a lemming and just going along with the crowd.

But my willful, opinionated nature is also my Achilles' heel; it is a weakness that has gotten me into hot water again and again. I tend to question EVERY authority and every point of view that is different from my own! I have difficulty letting go of my way of seeing the world and making room for other opinions. And I tend to push away people who don't hold my view of the world. So, the idea of allowing for different opinions and points of view can be a bit of a challenge for me.

Accept, Reject… or Allow?

Figuring out how to stop rejecting or accepting experiences and just allow life to unfold is an issue that I will probably struggle with and learn about my entire life. What exactly does it mean to "allow?" Being in allowance means I don't try to embrace or fight against people or experiences anymore. I can relax and allow events to be however they are WITHOUT feeling the need to accept or reject them.

Accepting or rejecting things takes a ton of time and energy. And acceptance vs. rejection is such a polarized black and white way of approaching the world. It's the view that everyone and everything is right or wrong, good or bad. The two energies are actually just flip sides of the same coin.

Allowance takes me beyond holding rigid black and white opinions about the world. Allowance gives me a third choice; a middle path.

And being in a state of allowance is so different from the polarized, right / wrong energy of accepting vs. rejecting. Allowance is a calm, open space of no judgment; a space where nothing need be labeled right or wrong, good or bad. Everyone and everything is just "allowed" to be however they are today. No need to agree or disagree with that person, just allow space for them to be different. No need to accept or reject that newscast predicting doom and gloom; just breathe and allow for many different ways of seeing the same events.

Being in allowance is like a revelation for me! The idea of just allowing the world outside of me to be however it is today – the idea that I do NOT have to align with it or push against things is a HUGE shift.

Allowance shifts me out of agreeing or disagreeing with people and events. Being in allowance means that when a person has a different opinion than mine; I don't have to fight to change their mind or push them away! I can just "allow" that their way of seeing the world is very different from mine.

Allowance is at the heart of the middle path that Buddha spoke of. I think that it's also the space of non-judgment that Christ preached about in so many of his sermons. And it's the place a wise Sufi wrote so eloquently about. It's the space of allowing life to be just as it is.

> *"Out beyond ideas of wrong-doing and right-doing,*
> *there is a field. I'll meet you there."*
>
> *~Rumi*

Saying Goodbye

Author's Note: I wrote this essay a few months before my dad died.

My dad is 85 and lives in a locked nursing home unit. He is locked in because my mom is fading away with Alzheimer's and my dad cannot wrap his head around the idea of letting her go. Dad literally cannot conceive of allowing her to go without him. He has had multiple strokes as his body and mind fight against the inevitable.

Dad obsesses about my mom's deterioration, he yells at her and even smacks her because she no longer knows who he is. All of this craziness comes from a calm, gentle soul who adores his wife. This from a man who rarely raised his voice before my mom got sick. Now Dad tries to guard my mom. He constantly worries that someone on the nursing home staff will hurt her or kill her. His behavior has gotten so bad, that my siblings and I reluctantly moved him to a locked unit. Now Dad rarely gets to see the love of his life.

This move has been another heartbreak for Dad. And it is heartbreaking for me to watch. Now that he has been separated from my mom, he is rapidly deteriorating physically. This man who never took medications and was always strong and tough as nails is fading fast now that his last job – the job of protecting his wife – has ended.

I sat with my dad as he slept this weekend. I watched him sleep and thought about everything that he has been through. My dad is strong willed and tenacious; he doesn't give up easily. As a young man, he pushed and worked and became the first person in his family to go to college. Then he pushed and he worked and he became an award-winning engineer with patents in his name. He pushed and he worked and he went much further than even his parents dreamed he could go. And then life threw something at him that only got worse when he pushed against it. Life threw something at him that demanded surrender and allowance.

I have not seen my dad for about 6 weeks, and there has been a big shift in his appearance and his behavior; he has transformed in just a few short weeks. He has stopped trying to halt my mom's deterioration. He has finally stopped pushing. He has let go.

I sat and looked at my dad's body that has aged so much in just a few weeks. I sat with Dad and watched his peaceful face as he slept. I sat with Dad, and I knew that he would soon let go completely; he will leave this body and this life that had become so painful for him. I sat with Dad and I cheered him on; YES! Let go, Dad. Surrender. Allow life to be however it is. Let go and leave all this pain behind.

This could be a story about the pain of love lost or the harsh realities of aging and dying in America today. My Dad's past few years have overflowed with both of those things. But for me, this is a lesson in how life can deteriorate into pain and pure misery if I grasp at it and try to hold it still.

My Dad's story has shown me what can happen if I resist and refuse to flow with whatever life throws at me. It is a warning about creating huge problems and pain whenever we choose to resist the change that is an inevitable part of life.

Dad, I hope you can leave this painful place soon. Let go and go. I will miss you so AND it's OK to go now.

Flow

When I get impatient with myself or with the world, I try to pause long enough to remember the river, the flow of the river that I love so much.

When life does not instantly present me with the exact and perfect outcome – the perfect and glorious outcome I had all planned out in my head in excruciating detail – at those times, I try to remember to just breathe and flow with how things ARE, rather than how I wish they would be.

Resistance is futile; life is NEVER perfect. And life unfolds in its own wild and wonderful way, no matter how hard I kick and scream and struggle and fight against what IS, trying desperately to get the exact future I had imagined and dreamed of.

Sit and breathe. And breathe some more. Sit and breathe until I can stop whining and fighting against what is unfolding right here and now in front of me. How horrible to miss out on today because it doesn't look exactly like my dream of it yesterday!

Leave Muck Behind

Where am I holding on to old ways of being that no longer work?

Where am I holding on to old mistakes and muck that weigh me down?

Today I choose to leave my muck behind and go for the light.

The light is where Joy lives.

The light is where I Bloom.

The light is pure Love.

Just Right Goldilocks

My Dad passed away in the summer of 2013. And lately, I have many memories coming up about him; things he said and did, what I loved about him and also a few things I didn't like so much. One of my favorite memories is hearing him call me Goldilocks. Goldy or Goldilocks was my Dad's nickname for me. Even in his last days, when he was hurting and in bad shape, he would look up, smile and say, "It's Goldy!" whenever I walked into the room.

I liked being called Goldy. No one except my dad has ever called me that. So, the nickname passes on with my dad, which is a little sad. But I had many years of being called Goldy or Goldilocks, and the name still makes me smile.

Goldy actually referred to the golden blonde hair I had as a child. But Dad also used the name because he said, like Goldilocks, I would search and try out new things until I found the one that was "just right". So true, so true! I still do that. Apparently I was picky and unwilling to settle even as a young girl.

I still search and push to find that one "just right" thing. I have found amazing houses to live in because of my constant quest for "just right". And I love finding just the right restaurant, hiking trail, lawn chair or vacation spot. Searching for "just right" also led me to shift careers and try a lot of different jobs until I zeroed in on a profession that truly suits me. And my inner life is so much richer because of all the spiritual traditions I have explored over the years while searching for one that was just right for me.

But searching for "just right" can also be problematic. I have to be careful that my "just right" search doesn't degenerate into a search for perfection. Yes, there is a difference between perfect and "just right". Perfect has an obsessive-compulsive energy to it. When I get locked in perfect mode, it feels absolutely necessary to attain perfection.

I sometimes get sucked into searching for the perfect word or phrase when I am writing. And I feel compelled to keep trying and trying long after a reasonable person would quit. I can waste a ton of energy and make myself completely miserable when I fall into perfect mode.

The search for "just right" is more relaxed than perfection – there's nothing necessary about finding "just right." In the fairytale Goldilocks could sleep in any of those beds – she just wants to optimize her comfort! So what if Goldy spends a few extra minutes trying out every bed. There's nothing OCD about it. "Just right" is about exploring all the options. "Just right" is nice to have, but not necessary.

My Dad is gone now, off exploring in other realms. But while he was here with me, he taught me a lot about life and myself. I am so grateful to have had him as my Dad.

And I love that Dad found my quest for "just right" interesting and amusing. Another parent might have turned this personality trait of mine into a big problem. But Dad embraced my "just right" quirkiness. I love remembering that.

Safe travels Dad. May your doors and gates and paths be open.

Dancing with Dad

""Your joy is your sorrow unmasked. And the selfsame well from which your laughter rises was oftentimes filled with your tears. And how else can it be? The deeper that sorrow carves into your being, the more joy you can contain."

~Kahlil Gibran

My dad struggled to hang on and stay here long past the point of misery, so his passing was a relief in many ways. But there are still days when I have images of him in my head all day, and I miss him a lot. And other days I don't think of him at all. Grief is a strange beast.

This morning I remembered a time many years ago when my dad tried to teach me how to jitterbug. Tried is the operative word here – I never could hold my torso still and get my feet to do what his were doing so perfectly. In my defense, I am not known for my coordination. Besides, I had a glass of wine before the dance instruction began!

Dad loved to tell people the tale of how his Navy buddy taught him to jitterbug. I always loved that story; Dad had joined the Navy at 18 and shipped out to California for basic training just as WWII ended. He went from a tiny town in southern Illinois to suddenly being in the Navy on a ship with hundreds of other guys. I imagine that it was all quite a shock for a young geeky country boy. One of his older shipmates took my dad under his wing. He helped my dad settle in to life in the Navy. And he also taught Dad how to jitterbug so he could impress the ladies.

I love the image of my skinny 18 year-old Dad with his baby face, dressed in baggy jeans and a work shirt, dancing the jitterbug with some big beefy guy in the tightly cramped quarters of a battleship! LOL - Life truly is stranger than fiction. The dance lessons definitely paid off because 40 years later my dad was still an amazing dancer.

I miss Dad. I wish I had danced with him more. This morning, as I flashed on images of the handful of times that we danced together, I heard Dad's voice in my ear. He said, "We'll dance again." And I suddenly saw an image of two energies dancing and flowing together and then apart, together and then apart. And as the energies danced, they morphed and changed shape, but I could tell that it was still the energy of Dad and I dancing together.

I think that image of my energy dance with Dad is actually a great lesson about the rhythm of life and death. We are energies that come together to dance on Earth, then part in death. Then we will come together again in a new place and dance a new dance. Over and over, we dance together in one form or another.

Later in the morning, I hike up one of my favorite trails, still thinking about my dad and missing him. I stop on a mesa to rest awhile. As I sit under the pines writing, I am startled by a hawk's cry above me. I look up and see two hawks soaring and spiraling just above my rocky perch. The hawks appear to be dancing together on the wind. It is a beautiful dance.

Another memory surfaces as I watch the hawks; I flash on the image of my dad dancing with my mom. In my memory, they are both in their late sixties and have been together for over 40 years. When they danced together, they were so closely in synch that it was like watching a single body move and flow to the music.

The hawks are gone when I next look up from my writing. But two young deer soon stumble upon my hiding place. They freeze for a moment. But when they realize that I won't harm them, they relax and forage for food a few feet behind me. Life dances on all around me.

I love you Dad. And I miss you. I miss your wide-open country boy smile. I miss your stories. I just plain miss you! But I know in my heart it was time for you to move on. And I am ok – I know that you and I will dance together again soon.

Resistance is Futile

Change is inevitable. Nothing stays the same for very long.

I take the same trail beside the river almost every day, and yet it is never quite the same path two days in a row. One morning last week on the trail, I found myself surrounded by trees on fire with autumn color. A few mornings later, snow completely blanketed the flaming trees and the sights and sounds of winter engulfed me.

Life is filled with cycles and shifts. From the passing of seasons to the aging of my body, change surrounds and engulfs me. And life continues to shift and change every day, every month, every year. Grasping at the old form and resisting change, makes today hurtful rather than joyful. I learned this lesson the hard way; years ago I owned a property in the Midwest that I loved. I adored every inch of those 3 acres – every tree, every blooming bush, every blade of grass was special to me. The property was so significant and special to me that I wrote an entire book about the place - my first book, _A Still Place_.

And there was nothing bad or wrong about my love of that little parcel of land. The only problem was that I clung to it and vowed to live in that spot until I died. Silly, silly woman! Well, life happened; I got divorced from one man and married another. I had a second baby and still I held onto that property. I refused to even think about moving. Then my husband's job dried up and we faced a move cross-country. And I had trouble letting go; I resisted leaving my lovely little property. But we needed to move! The only thing my resistance caused was a slow, slow house sale and a ton of pain and angst.

We eventually sold the property and moved 700 miles away. I was so sad, missing my little plot of land, wishing things were different, wanting to roll back the clock and undo the move. But gradually, I let go. And when I finally stopped holding onto my past, I "woke up" and discovered that I was living in an amazing spot. I found myself LOVING this new place and my new life. All it took was letting go of the old life.

That experience left me knowing that my life is WAY less painful when I allow things to change and shift without resisting or pushing against the change. Resistance is futile! Resisting change only leads to pain and misery.

I seem to periodically have to revisit this lesson in letting go and allowing life to unfold organically. I can still make myself miserable trying to force today to look like some "perfect" day long past – or some fantasy day that I've never even experienced. I can be so stubborn! But when I remember that little piece of land that I adored so many years ago, I remember the value of letting go.

It is very odd; I still have so many fond memories of that little plot of land. But now, I also remember all the amazing and wonderful stuff that happened to me when I let it go and moved on with my life. And you know what? Today, I live in a space that is even more amazing! And I would have never ended up here, if I hadn't let go of that old place.

Life is a river; it keeps flowing and changing and moving. And in every moment I have a choice; I can cling to the riverbank and wear myself out trying to stay right here in this spot.

I can fight and resist moving downstream. Or I can let go and allow the flow of life to take me. I can let go and trust that life can be even better around the next bend.

Can I stop resisting and be grateful for change?

Can I let go of my urge to control and push and grasp?

Can I allow life to unfold and be as it is?

Question Everything
Judge Nothing

"Only in an open, nonjudgmental space
can we acknowledge what we are feeling.
Only in an open space where we're not all caught up
in our own version of reality
can we see and hear and feel who others really are"

~Pema Chodron

More, More, More

Decorations in red and green hang on the walls. Christmas carols play softly in the background. And no matter where I turn, I see an advertisement for something that someone believes I really must buy. Candy, toys, books, music, clothes, gourmet coffee, electronic gadgets – the selection is endless. Buy me! Buy me! Every TV ad, every store, every restaurant and every street corner beckons with yet another item that I must buy to make my holiday complete. The ads would have me believe that happiness is just a quick purchase away.

I am such a good little consumer; I can feel myself getting sucked into the holiday buying frenzy. Every year I succumb to holiday fever and spend myself silly. I act totally wacko when it comes to my kids. I spend hours searching for the one item that each of my children is begging for. And eventually I find it and buy it. But buying that one special gift is not enough. I buy a few extra items… and then a few more… and a few more. I am the queen of spontaneous purchases – "Oh, isn't that cute! Maybe I'll get one of those too." On and on I go until my charge card is smoking from overuse and I can't begin to remember everything I've purchased. And I do all of this with the heartfelt desire of creating a very special Christmas for my family.

But I am beginning to have the sneaking suspicion that creating a special Christmas for my family has nothing to do with buying more stuff. I have been noticing that all of this "stuff" does not seem to make any of us happier. Oh sure, I get a little thrill from my new suede shoes. But the joy fades quickly. And in the end I am still the same content or discontent soul I was before I bought those new shoes.

Is buying more "stuff" the path to happiness? Do I really believe that I can buy a happy holiday? Is it just that I haven't found the store that has my happy holiday stocked in the correct size and color?

In the book, _How to Want What You Have,_ Timothy Miller writes that most Americans are consumed with having more - more money, more status, more stuff. We are never satisfied with where we are or what we have right now. We want more, more, more. And the wanting leaves us miserable.

It may be downright un-American to say this, but enough is enough! Happy holidays cannot be found in any mall. All this buying just leaves me with more bills to pay and more stuff to store and clean and take care of. This Christmas I want to change my ways. No more over-limit charge cards and buyer's remorse in January.

That old saying "Out of sight, out of mind" applies here. I have stopped browsing through the catalogs that flood my mailbox. And I studiously ignore TV commercials. These simple actions have dramatically diminished my "I need one of those" list. If I don't see it, I don't obsess and ruminate about how much is lacking in my life because I don't own it.

It is still weeks until Christmas and I feel like a warrior preparing for battle. Fortitude! I can do this! Turn off that radio come-on. Avoid that mall. Think long and hard about what each person on my list really wants. Plan quick shopping forays when my endurance is at its highest. And a pat on the back for every day that passes without a crazy purchase.

It is hard work swimming against the tide of a consumer Christmas. Every ad is designed to whet my buying appetite. But when it gets hard fighting the "more, more, more" mindset, I focus on some things that I really do want more of this holiday: more hugs, more laughter, more quiet fun with friends and family, more joy and inner peace. None of those are for sale at my local mall. I plan to make them myself this year.

Do Spiritual Masters Get Triggered?

Emotion is as natural for humans as breathing.
I don't make my breathing right or wrong,
why do it with my emotions?

It's been an interesting week; I have spent more time than I care to remember in my swamp. By swamp I mean a sticky, tangled, mess of uncomfortable emotions within myself. I don't like my emotional swamp much – a lot of what I experience in the swamp sucks – it hurts. And then I add to my pain by judging myself for feeling this sticky, yucky crap in the first place. I would love to avoid my swamp.

Isn't life supposed to turn into bliss and pure joy when I open up to more consciousness? Have I failed because I still get triggered after all these years of awareness training? Am I doing this consciousness thing wrong if I still get pissed and sad and scared?

But, wait a minute! All humans emote about their experiences – even beings as aware as Gandhi and Jesus felt emotions. Our bodies are wired to flow with emotion. Emotion is as natural for humans as breathing. I don't make my breathing right or wrong, so why do it with my emotions?

Every experience I have can trigger emotional reactions, not just the yummy experiences. Where did I get the idea that becoming conscious meant never being triggered, never feeling "yucky" emotions? Isn't that just a really sneaky way to judge myself and find myself lacking? Just what I need – another way to beat myself up and make myself bad or wrong. NOT!

And what if being more aware in each moment elicits even more emotion within me? All those sensations about this moment that I used to block or ignore are now available to me in my new state of awareness. What if those sensations trigger MORE emotions as I respond to all the new information I am now aware of? Is that somehow wrong?

And isn't it just another form of judgment to label emotions good or bad, acceptable or repulsive? How is it going to help me to label my emotions as OK and not OK? Can I let go of the idea that some human emotions are a sign of unconsciousness or inferiority?

Humans are emotional creatures. Trying to stop emotion is like trying to halt the flow of water. Can I allow my emotions to flow without stuffing them? And can I stop judging myself right or wrong for feeling the way I feel in each moment?

What happens if I embrace it all – my grief, my anger, my fear? Can I allow my emotions to be waves washing through me? What happens if I embrace ALL of me – even the parts I don't like – in every moment?

"It's not that you won't be triggered anymore.
It's that you won't have a problem being triggered anymore."

~Panache Desai

Maybe Good, Maybe Bad

We Live in a World of Duality

Form & Formless

Life & Death

Light & Dark

Physical & Ethereal

Good & Bad

Moon & Sun

Female & Male

Right & Wrong

Love & Hate

Sorrow & Joy

Yin & Yang

The energy of our Universe flows and dances constantly between tangible form and formless energy. I am part of an intricate weaving of light and dark, form and formless, growth and decay. Duality is woven into the very fabric of this Universe. And duality is a natural part of the miraculous dance of Spirit within earth, air, fire and water.

How do I keep my balance within this ever-shifting duality?

Pain and problems arise when I turn duality into polarity – when I attach an emotional charge to a person or an event. I may label something **bad** and reject it... or decide someone else is **wrong** and I am **right**... or push an experience away as **bad** and **unwanted**... or desperately crave something I don't have.

Pain and disconnect are inevitable whenever I polarize my experiences into good and bad, right and wrong.

Judging EVERY single experience as good or badonly makes me crazy and miserable!

What if I stop judging and labeling every aspect of Life as good or bad, right or wrong? What if I stop living in a state of charged polarity? What if I choose to actually live by the wisdom of the Tao?

"If good happens, good;
if bad happens, good. "

~Lao Tzu, Tao Te Ching

I want to share one of my favorite parables about good and bad:

A farmer had only one stallion. One day, the horse jumped a fence and ran away. All the neighbors came by saying, "Oh no! Such bad luck! You must be so upset." The man just said, "Maybe good, maybe bad – too soon to tell."

A few days later, his stallion came back and brought twenty wild mares with him. The man and his son corralled all the horses. All the neighbors came by saying, "Wow! This is such good news. You must be so happy!" The man just said, "Maybe good, maybe bad – too soon to tell."

A few weeks later, one of the wild horses kicked the man's only son, and broke the boy's leg in 3 places. All the neighbors came by saying, "I'm so sorry. This is such bad news. You must be so upset." The man just said, "Maybe good, maybe bad – too soon to tell."

A month later, the country went to war, and every able-bodied young man was drafted to fight. The war was terrible and killed many young men from the region, but the farmer's son was spared; his broken leg prevented him from fighting.

All the neighbors came by saying, "You are so lucky! Your son didn't have to go fight" The man just said, "Maybe good, maybe bad – too soon to tell."

~Author Unknown

*What if I stop judging all of my experiences
and how I handle them?*

*What if I meet EVERY singly experience with the energy of
maybe good, maybe bad – too soon to tell?"*

Spirit already has everything under control, no matter how it looks in this moment. Maybe I should just open up and embrace the natural and inevitable duality of this world.

*Can I stop judging and polarizing everything that happens to
me?*

*What if I allow my world to be however it happens to be
today?*

To allow is not polarized; to allow is a loose, easy state where I am open to possibilities. When I relax and *allow* my life to unfold, peace fills me. And balance follows.

Clueless

*Ever have a day when you realize that you don't have a clue
what the 'right' answer is?*

When did I decide that I am supposed to figure it all out?

When I let go and finally surrender to not knowing, a huge
lightness opens up in me. Not knowing opens up a gorgeous new
way to *Be*.

And it's very scary to admit I don't have the answer, don't know
what to do…

Breathe and let go of my need to figure it all out
No answer is required
Just stay in the wondering.

The Illusion of Perfection

Everybody wants perfect health, right? No more physical ailments, no more pain. We each crave a perfectly shaped body that silently and efficiently does whatever we demand of it. But is that even possible?

Life is about finding a balance point between opposing forces; to stay alive, I must strike a balance between motion and stillness, between liquid fluidity and grounded earthy stability, between shadow and light, between creative and destructive forces. The world is constantly shifting and changing around us; temperatures rise and fall, one day it rains, the next is sunny. My body is designed to constantly shift and change as well.

Origin of the word Heal

Haelan (Olde English)
to Heal is to bloom, to embody wholeness
to feel complete, to be in balance

This idea of health being a dynamic balancing act becomes obvious when I look at natural environments. Balanced nature is never static; healthy ecosystems are diverse and contain many elements that constantly interact with each other. And the entire natural system finds balance through an ongoing dance between the elements; water wears down stone and sweetens the dirt with minerals that the trees use to grow. And the trees on the riverbank draw river water up into their bodies and in doing so, slow down and calm the river's wild currents. The trout rest in the shade of the trees, waiting for bugs to get blown into the current by the wind and become dinner. True balance lies in the web of interactions between bug and wind, fish and tree, stone and water.

What if there is no perfect physical state that I can attain
and be 'finished' or 'complete'?

I look again at nature – *Nothing* is perfect in nature; tree trunks are crooked spirals, flowers are not symmetrical, and each animal has little quirks and imperfections in its shape; eyes are slightly different sizes, ears are uneven, spots are imperfect or missing. Perfection is a human delusion; it does not exist in nature.

It is a waste of time and energy to strive for perfection. Perfect for what moment, what situation? Healthy balance is a wobbly, imperfect and dynamic process; much like riding a bicycle requires continuous tweaks and changes to stay upright, so does my body cycle through continuous shifts and changes in order to stay in balance. I do myself a huge disservice when I reject and judge and try to annihilate my issues and imperfections.

Balance and healing will elude me
until I can surrender to imperfection and constant change.

True healing is about allowing myself to be complete just as I am in this moment, warts, bad hair, temper tantrums and all. In the end, healing is not a "fix my faults" project. And it's not about finding someone to help me change or improve either. True healing is about learning to wholeheartedly love and embrace the wonderfully quirky, imperfect, amazing and unique creatures I already am.

My Box

*I live my life in a box – everyone does.
My box may be a sacred box or a profane box,
but it is still a box.*

I have created a box or a "comfort zone" in life where I spend my days and feel safe. It is a mental box that I created from all the rules and habits that define where I live and work, who I interact with, what's acceptable, "safe" behavior, what's allowed in my family and my culture, what's bad or wrong behavior, etc. And all those things that I have decided are off-limits, too big or too scary to be part of my life, create the walls of my box.

Pain and Boredom as Catalysts

Ultimately my box defines how much of my true self I will share with the world. It's very hard to be a big presence in the world if I choose to inhabit a tiny little box. But my little comfort zone of a box provides continuity and safety for me – no one wants to live in a completely unpredictable world where everything is new and unknown all the time. And my little box may be beautiful and fun for me. But as time passes my comfortable little box of a life may come to feel constrictive and limiting; I may begin to feel caged up and ache for something new.

The most amazing box can ultimately become downright painful; mine certainly did in the months before I decided to get divorced from my first husband. Or I might inhabit the same comfortable box for so long and come to know every corner of it so well, and then find myself bored to tears by its predictability. That was the case for several years before I chose to completely shift gears and change careers.

When I am bored or in pain, I am way more willing to stretch and embrace a little of the unknown. And I am way more likely to seek out change. I may decide to take a class, go on a trip, change jobs, start exercising, change my diet... I took a huge leap and got divorced from my first husband – but only after aching for a change for years. I am only human; change, big change is most likely to happen when my box becomes too painful or too boring to bear for another second.

Pushing My Limits

Every shift or change I have ever made, involves expansion; I end up pushing against the limits of my old comfort zone. And like most people, I am willing to wait a long time and put up with a lot of boredom or pain before I try to change my life. It's great to feel safe and comfortable. And change can be very uncomfortable and scary. But when my box becomes too painful or restrictive, I eventually reach an internal tipping point. Then I am willing to swallow my trepidation and make a change in my life.

With every change, I inevitably run up against my old limits; I push up against the walls of the safe and known box I've been living in. Or if I shift fast, I may even completely blow through the walls of my box before I realize it!

When I run into, or completely blow by my old familiar limits, I feel fear – it's not very comfortable to be outside my old box at first. And I am likely to find ways to contract again and sabotage myself. I get shaky and try to talk myself out of the shift. Or I decide I can't handle the change or don't know how to change. Ever insecurity of mine rears its ugly head!

Craving and Sabotaging Change

When I feel shaky, it's natural to want to crawl right back inside my old box; to run back to my old comfort zone, even when a huge part of me is aching and crying out for something bigger, something more. But I've learned that it helps me immensely to remember that whenever I grow and expand, I will knock up against the walls of the comfortable "box" I've been living in. And when I do, I will feel quite vulnerable and fearful. It's part of the process.

I find it comforting to realize that I am just being human whenever I get scared and sabotage my own growth and change. I may even give myself a little slack if I can remember that all of us tend to do stupid, self-defeating things when we're in a new world and feel off-balance and scared.

Realizing that it's human nature to both crave and resist change helps me relax and offer myself some grace. When I can own that part of me that fears and fights against change, it is much easier to catch myself whenever I start to contract back into my safe little box.

"Do one thing every day that scares you."

~Eleanor Roosevelt

Don't Pitch a Tent in Hell

Years ago, I heard an idea in a sermon that really touched me. It has stuck with me for years. The minister said, "If you're in hell, DON'T pitch a tent! Keep moving!" I love the visual image in that – that image fills me with the energy of get up and go! Don't just sit there – do something! Move!

That idea of keep moving, don't pitch a tent in Hell, comes back to me now as I think about choice and the power in choosing. How often have I sat, locked up and unable to choose something? How long did I sit there in discomfort or pain – "in hell" – unable to choose, unable to move? And what exactly keeps me locked up and sitting in Hell, unable or unwilling to move? Well, for me, it's usually fear that I will choose the wrong thing.

"Choose the wrong thing" – whew, can you feel the weight of that? Choose the wrong thing – make a "bad" choice – mess up. Wow, so instead of choosing anything, I will sit in pain and discomfort and discontent. I will pitch a tent and stay in my personal version of Hell. Being wrong – choosing the wrong thing has a HUGE heavy, yucky energy to it. Do I actually abhor being wrong so much that I will sit in pain and disease; that I will pitch a tent in Hell?!

When did choosing become so heavy and serious and difficult? Do little kids have difficulty choosing and keeping moving? Heck no! Try stopping a 2 year old from choosing – and choosing again – and again – and again! Kids are like sharks; in a constant state of motion and choosing all the time. Kids stay in choice and keep moving no matter what. Do they sit down and contemplate that last choice they made to grab that toy and whap their brother upside the head with it? No way! Do they stop and beat themselves up about how bad they are, what a bad choice that was? No way!

Little kids definitely notice and log it whenever they choose something that gets them in trouble or ends up hurting, but they do NOT sit down and contemplate their wrong-ness and the error of their ways like I do! We have been trained to ruminate on our wrong-ness.

So, when did I decide that each choice I make is so critical and so loaded with "don't mess up and make the wrong choice" energy that I better slow down, stop moving and contemplate each choice for hours or days? And does that way of being in the world serve me? Doesn't stopping to analyze every choice from every possible angle just keep me sitting in Hell longer?

How can I choose faster and easier? How can I unlock choosing, take the weight out of it, so that next time I'm in a painful, hellish place I don't get stuck there?! How can I make choices more like a kid – or with the energy of an explorer? Did Lewis and Clark sit and contemplate which path to choose for days? Heck no, they kept moving or they would have never made it to the Pacific Ocean!

I would like to get back into that childlike energy of choosing. That "let's try this and see what happens. And if it doesn't work out, no big deal – I'll just choose something different" frame of mind. How can I do that? Is that possible at my age? Why not?

I want to start moving through life like a kid exploring. And to do that, I going to have to stop criticizing and judging every single choice I make. THAT's what gets me stuck – that critical, look what a "bad" choice you made energy.

Funny, as I write this, that critical voice surfaces in my head, saying,

> *"Oh Nancy, this entire piece is just stupid. And nobody is going understand what you are trying to say anyway. So, why bother? Just delete this drivel and go do something safe."*

Whew, man that is some heavy, yucky energy! THAT is the energy of being wrong, isn't it? But you know what? I'm going to choose to blow off that yucky nasty critical voice and publish this anyway.

I choose to publish this book even though it may be incoherent or incomplete or not quite right. I choose to put this out there anyway. I'm going to choose and choose and choose again.

Am I a Good Witch or a Bad Witch?

What Else is Possible Here? Why do I have to be either good or bad? What if I am both a good witch AND a bad witch, depending on the day?

And when did I decide that women are supposed to be sorted into good or bad, saint or sinner? When did I conclude that I am either an innocent pure Madonna or a conniving evil whore?

I blame my messed up need to decide whether I'm good or evil on too many Disney movies... and I'm only half kidding! I challenge you to name one female Disney character that is not some ridiculous caricature of pure good or pure evil. And no, you CANNOT count the female dog in Lady and the Tramp! I'm talking about female HUMANS in Disney movies – name one – I dare you. Consider Snow White and her nemesis, the Evil Queen. How about Cinderella and her Evil stepmother? Or there's Ariel and the Evil Octopus Lady Ursula. We are talking some seriously twisted black and white views of women!

Or maybe I should blame it on my Christian upbringing. But wait a minute... those are ALL bad, evil woman images aren't they? Eve, Lilith, Salome, whorish Mary Magdalene. The only good female image I can come up with after spending years of Sunday school is Mother Mary, and she is merely used as a vessel brought in to birth the baby Jesus. Then she exits quickly stage left. The Bible expresses a pretty dark view of my gender.

But it's not just women getting labeled all good or all bad. The entire world seems to obsess about sorting everyone and every experience into good or bad, right or wrong, black or white. We love to polarize! Watch what the politicians say about each other and you'll see exactly what I mean.

At the Republican Convention, every speaker praised Mitt Romney as our national savior and vilified Barack Obama as the evil anti-Christ. Meanwhile, at the Democratic Convention, Obama wore the white hat and Romney was depicted in black. What if BOTH images are just silly theatrics? What happens when we realize that BOTH candidates are just mere mortal men? What if they are normal human beings with both strengths and weaknesses? What if we just stopped buying into this black and white bullshit?

If you hate politics, just watch a little reality TV and notice how black and white it is. The Kardashian sisters appear to spend every waking moment fighting about which of them is the good-est witch and which is the baddest! Even the son-in-laws get sorted into good (Lamar) and evil (Scott). It is so polarized and so divisive. But it makes for tons of drama. And I just cannot seem to look away.

What if I just stopped playing the polarity game? What if I chose to see the world as a thousand different shades rather than just black or white? Blow that black and white mindset up! It only makes me crazy and upset anyway.

Ok, so what if I embrace both my good witch AND my bad witch? Everyone who knows me will tell you I am quite capable of being both – and sometimes even in the same day. What if I just relax and stop judging myself as GOOD or BAD, RIGHT or WRONG? And what if I stop judging everyone else too? What might happen then?

"Glinda, the Good Witch: Are you a good witch, or a bad witch?

Dorothy: I'm not a witch at all. I'm Dorothy Gale from Kansas.

Glinda: Oh. Well, is that the witch?

Dorothy: Who, Toto? Toto's my dog!"

~The Wizard of Oz

A Space of No Judgment

Do flowers sit around judging how well they are blooming today?

Does a baby berate herself about how much she cries?
Or how loud she laughs?

Does the wind worry about upsetting me with its strength?

Can I learn to live in a space of no judgment?

If flowers and babies and the wind can do it, why can't I?

A Walk in the Woods

"Said the river: imagine everything you can imagine,
then keep on going."

~Mary Oliver

I went for a walk in the woods a few days ago. I love paths that are
a bit wild and natural even in the middle of town. On this particular
day, I was on one of my favorite trails; the path meanders through a
dense patch of woods next to a big wide creek. This trail has been
left untouched for decades in many places and I love wandering
here. But walking into some sections of this trail brings to
mind Dorothy hesitantly walking into the dark scary woods with
the scarecrow on her journey to Oz. Or maybe it's Gretel wandering
in the forest with Hansel, looking for her way home. Either way, the
path can be a bit unnerving. I find myself humming that old Lou
Reed song, "Walk on the Wild Side", as I walk.

Deep dark untamed woods hold big, scary, archetypal energy for
me and lots of other people; all those wild, uncivilized natural
spaces where we might just meet something bigger and hungrier
than us on the path. It is exciting and enticing and scary all at once.

Is that why our ancestors spent so much time trying to tame Mother
Nature? Generation after generation of Americans have spent huge
amounts of time and energy trying to corral and control Mother
Nature; clearing away the forests that once covered the northeastern
U.S. like they were tidying up a closet by throwing almost
everything away. And the U.S. Army Corps of Engineers dredged
and straightened and pushed around the Mississippi river decade
after decade – we all saw how well that worked out for New
Orleans when Hurricane Katrina made mincemeat of the Corps'
dykes.

Otherwise logical and reasonable adults plant grass over mile after
mile of suburban neighborhoods, then burn thousands of hours of
free time and gallons of gasoline every weekend mowing their

lawns down with military precision. All because somebody decided it was important to force grass to be a "tidy" length that resembles some perfectly uniform man-made carpet. We humans cannot seem to leave Mother Nature to her own devices, can we?

Mother Nature scares the crap out of most humans. Most of us hide out in our man-made homogenized suburban boxes and pretend Nature doesn't exist. Or we head out loaded for bear to try and kick Mother Nature's butt and make her our bitch. In the end, neither way works very well.

I go visit an old tree every time I walk this path. Her diameter is larger than my wingspan. I remember the golden mean ratio – exactly how tall does that trunk diameter mean she is? And how many rings does her trunk hold? Her rings must carry the wisdom and the history of this place at the edge of the path, this spot that she has anchored for at least 80 years. This tree has been here at the edge of this path for many, many years; she has seen all this human silliness before.

That's where true wisdom comes from, being as silent and still as an old tree; just absorbing what happens in whatever place I find myself today. And in taking the time to make the connections between what happens today and what happened yesterday on my path – and 2 years ago and 200 years ago. I need to remember to stop and get still; to watch and listen to everything happening around me. And to take the time to reflect, to remember and store that long view of history like an old tree does.

I leave grandma tree and move on down the path. As I wander, I look up at the sky and realize that a storm is rapidly brewing on the horizon; it's time to head for the safety of my house. Once home, I sit by the window in my study and watch the wind and rain thrash at the trees. Lightning splits the sky again and again. Mother Nature is flexing her muscles. Even my tame garden seems a bit scary now. I watch the storm from a safe perch inside.

The path I choose again and again is not tame and civilized like a perfectly groomed suburban lawn. But it's also not a solitary cabin surrounded by wilderness; I don't require a life so wild and scary that I quiver with fear like the cowardly lion every time I venture out into the world.

I seem to constantly be searching for the middle path; in my mind I picture land on the boundary between wild woods and tame suburbs. That feels like the space where I belong. It is the space where I feel most at home.

There has to be a way of living that is more in synch with my own inner nature. I want be find that way, to dig in and explore that middle path. I wonder if it is possible to live in way that is engaged with Mother Nature, fascinated and respectful of her powers rather than trying to subdue and mow and bend her to my will? And at the same time, can I develop a connection with Mother Nature so deep that I'm not left feeling completely helpless in her storms?

What is the middle path through this landscape? How do I become an actual friend and ally of Mother Nature? There are a thousand different opinions out there about how to walk softly on the earth; go vegan, buy local, grow your own, buy a hybrid, solar power… But I am wondering about diving deeper and making choices where I work with Mother Nature rather than doing things to her.

Whatever I choose has to come from my heart truly connecting with the natural world. I wonder what will my life look like if I open up and deeply connect with Mother Nature? What would it look like to be close friends with this Earth? This feels like a shifting my path… like rounding a bend on a trail and seeing a whole new vista opening up in front of me.

And just like any great adventure, this new terrain is exciting and a little scary, but not too scary…

"There is always more mystery."

~Anais Nin

Share Your Self

"Oh I can't keep it in,
I can't keep it in, I've gotta let it out.
I've got to show the world, world's got to see,
see all the love, love that's in me..."

~Cat Stevens

Tiny Trim Tab Ripples

When I look around me, the world appears to be quite a mess; news of fiscal cliffs, disasters and every kind of human and planetary suffering abound. I see a world teeming with negativity and fear. And many people seem to wallow in fear day after day with no way out.

If I allow myself to spiral into fear and worry, I can end up wallowing in pain and pessimism all day long. And when I get stuck in worry and fear, I can't help myself or anyone else; my personal angst only adds more pain to the world.

I am reminded of Buckminster Fuller's story. In his 30's, Buckminster became quite depressed about how his life was going. He felt guilty about how much he drank and how he had neglected his family. He felt like a complete failure and thought about killing himself. But one day, he asked himself if he had truly tried. And he decided to turn the rest of his life into an experiment.

"Something hit me very hard once, thinking about what one little man could do. Think of the Queen Mary — the whole ship goes by and then comes the rudder. And there's a tiny thing at the edge of the rudder called a trim tab. It's a miniature rudder. Just moving the little trim tab builds a low pressure that pulls the rudder around. Takes almost no effort at all.

So I said that the little individual can be a trim tab. Society thinks it's going right by you, that it's left you altogether. But if you're doing dynamic things mentally, the fact is that you can just put your foot out like that and the whole big ship of state is going to go. So I said, call me Trim Tab."

~Buckminster Fuller

Buckminster went on to become an internationally renowned designer. He decided that he could be a little trim tab and change the course of the world. And he made a huge difference. Little ripples matter.

Yes, much of this world is a complete and utter mess. How do I stay calm and keep our equilibrium when faced with such horrible news day after day? And how can one person possibly make a difference in a world that is so messed up? What is the point in even trying?

But in every moment that we wriggle free of all that energy of worry and fear – every moment free of that tangled web, is a moment to celebrate. Every moment that we can be peaceful is a little ripple of yummy energy sent out into the world.
And *every* little ripple of love and joy and peace that we create makes a difference.

Remember the power of the trim tab and the little ripples it makes that turn the Queen Mary around; little ripples of peace and joy and love and calmness matter whether we consciously realize it or not. Every little yummy ripple we create matters.

Advice to myself today: Breathe. And breathe again. Relax. And whenever possible, send a few ripples of peace or love or joy out into the world. Be a trim tab!

Making Ripples

I am thinking about ripples again today, tiny ripples. I throw a pebble into the pond and it sends out little ripples in all directions, spreading further and further in each moment. That one tiny action reverberates through the entire body of water.

I remember an article in Life Magazine that mentioned research done on premature babies; just 10 minutes of gentle touch per day led to dramatic weight gains and earlier hospital dismissals. As a nurse healer I am intimately familiar with the healing power of touch. Yet I continue to be amazed at how much just a gentle hand on a body can do. Amazing healing comes from just touching someone with love. Little actions make a big difference.

Gary Zukav's classic book, _Dancing Wu Li Masters_, speaks of the dance of energy that quantum physicists now study. These scientists have discovered that on a sub-atomic level, life is all about tiny particles dancing with each other in a vast empty space. It is the mythical Hindu creation dance of Shakti and Shiva rediscovered. At the sub-atomic level, nothing exists except particles dancing in relationship to each other. Everything is interconnected. That means my smallest action can ripple around the world in the blink of an eye.

This is the essence of Chaos Theory. You know the theory - a butterfly flapping its wings in South America can alter the weather pattern in Idaho. Chaos Theory sounded totally loony to me when I first read about it, but the more I practice energy work, the more I "get" how interconnected we all really are. Sometimes, when I get very still, I can feel invisible energy connecting me to another person. And sometimes I feel energy flows or currents between two beings. Is it so loony to believe that invisible energy threads connect us all together?

I listen to the news and it is filled with doom and gloom. The world seems to be going to Hell in a hand basket. Does one person getting shot or beaten or laid off from her job make the world more unsafe and inhospitable? Then a kind word or a few dollars sent to charity or a helping hand will make the world safer, more loving.

One loving gesture can alter the world. Every little choice I make to act from love instead of fear can and will reshape this world into the kind of place I want my children's children to live in. I want to remember that my actions can have consequences for my great-great-great-great grandchildren. Little ripples can have huge effects.

So, I guess that is my learning for today. Little actions matter; they matter a lot. Choose to act with love whenever possible and change the world. Spending just a few minutes really listening to another person can alter a life. Calling a sick friend to say I care may keep them going when it all seems hopeless. Sending a blessing instead of a curse after that kid that cuts me off in traffic might just alter his day – or my own. My thoughts and actions – your thoughts and actions - literally shape this world, one ripple at a time.

Change happens one person, one little action,
one moment at a time.

Fear of Bigness

"Our imagination flies; we are its shadow on the earth."

–Nabokov

Am I actually sharing just a shadow of my true self with the world? And isn't the part of me that I dare to share limited, pale and colorless compared to what I am capable of?! Why do I fear my true potency?

Marianne Williamson wrote about this so eloquently; our deepest fear is that we are powerful beyond measure. We fear being too big and bright in the world. We fear our BIG-ness, our potency.

What if I finally take the restraints off and show up in my entirety? What if the ONLY thing that will save this beautiful planet is choosing to be my Big, Gi-normous self, no matter what? No matter what others think, no matter what others say, no matter what others do, no matter how many "rules" I break in the process?

What will it take for me to STOP hiding out and playing small? What will it take for me to acknowledge and own ALL of my juicy BIG-ness?

And... what can happen to my world when I embrace my BIG-ness? What else is possible?

"Your divine impulse is yearning to emerge through the human you... In that shift, the more you embrace the Self, the Light, the more you surrender to your own light, the easier it is for you."

–Sai Maa

That Voodoo You Do

I am a seer; somehow I can sense or "see" what's beneath the surface of things. It is a gift that is bizarre and wonderful all at once.

My husband David likes to call my gift "that voodoo you do". Technically, it's not voodoo, but anything even remotely psychic is considered as weird as voodoo in this culture.

In the early days of opening up to my sight, we lived in a conservative Midwest neighborhood that was flanked by two very large, very traditional Christian churches. Being newly conscious of my sight, I would often blurt out something freaky that I had just 'seen' or dreamed, and my husband would laugh and say, "Be careful, they're going to burn you!"

It seems funny now, but just a few hundred years ago, his warning probably would have come true. Female seers scared the crap out of my Christian ancestors. Any woman who exhibited psychic abilities usually ended up getting burned at the stake or driven out of town. Even now, being a seer is not exactly considered a normal everyday skill.

But hey, who wants or be normal? That's what I used to tell my kids when they would moan about not being part of the popular crowd in grade school. What I did not share back then was that I did; I wanted to just be normal and fit in for most of my life.

I spent years suppressing my gift and pretending not to see. I denied my sight, just like my mother and her mother before her. But the sight was there, whether I wanted to acknowledge it or not.

Eventually I realized that refusing to 'see' was like cutting off my own hand or stabbing myself in the heart. Denying my truth was only guaranteed to make me suffer. And ultimately, only I can decide whether my sight is a blessing or a curse. It all depends on how I see myself.

I live on the edge of the mountains now, in a small town filled with mountain men, artists, mystics, and misfits. I write a lot; I teach once in a while. Some people call me a shaman, others say I'm a witch. My husband still teases me about being a voodoo queen.

But those are just silly labels. What's important is that I have finally relaxed into being myself, no matter what other people think. I have finally found a way of being in the world that works for me. My soul has come home.

Hold onto Self

How do I stay true to myself
as I move though this crazy world?

Can I keep flowing and resonating with my joy, my truth, even when surrounded by others who are awash in sorrow or fear or rage? How do I hold my ground and allow the world to be however it is today? I will not do any good to anyone if I drop my light, my joy and resonate with the pain of those around me.

Maybe it isn't cruel or crass to stay joyful while others in the world suffer. But what if our joy is the most potent medicine there is for the wounds of the world?

I want to acknowledge joy as the amazing gift it is. And to keep opening to joy, even in the face of the darkness and pain in the world around me.

May I hold my joy sacred and allow it to flow far and wide.

Lily expresses her essence fearlessly…
I doze in my hammock
Rocking in the warm summer breeze,
I dream that I bloom like Lily
I wake smiling.

Seek Joy

"Joy is the infallible sign of the presence of God."

~Teilhard de Chardin

Spacious Joy

Number of stars in the Milky Way galaxy: approximately
300,000,000,000.

Number of galaxies in this Universe: approximately 200,000,000,000

Wow!! There is obviously plenty of space in the Universe for me.
And more possibilities than my little human brain can fathom. Just
knowing that makes me smile.

Is it possible to be judgmental and spacious all at once? No way –
when I am spacious, my judgments seem to dissolve. Can I open up
to the gifts held within all that space? What can this immense
Universe offer me that I haven't even thought of yet?

Does the sky ever complain
that the mountain is hogging its space?

Can I be as spacious as the sky?

Today, I choose to be Spacious.

Spacious fills me with Joy.

Spa·cious / ˈspāSHəs/
Adjective
having ample space; capacious – roomy – wide – generous – ample – large -
extensive.

Recreation Pants

We have a "recreation pants" tradition at my house. What exactly are recreation pants, you ask? Think loungewear. Think pajama bottoms. Think baggy, comfortable and elastic!

Recreation pants go on at my house when it's time to leave the problems of the day behind. We will even announce to each other that it's time for recreation pants! It may sound silly to you, and it did actually start out as a joke. But the idea of putting on my recreation pants has come to mean much more to me.

"These are my recreation pants."

~Jack Black in Nacho Libre

The idea of recreation pants came to us after watching Jack Black ham it up in his irreverent and hilarious movie *Nacho Libre*. In the movie Nacho, AKA Jack Black, wants to impress the hot young nun (yes, I meant nun). So Nacho puts on his tight white stretch pants (think Saturday Night Fever pants). Then he poses against a pole and flexes his glutes for the nun. Seriously! It's a bit of Jack Black comedy genius.

At my house, recreation pants still make us smile, but it's not remotely about looking hot or impressing people; just the opposite. Around here, recreation pants are all about being relaxed and comfortable and not needing to impress anyone. Besides, who can look hot and sexy in old, baggy pajama bottoms anyway?

Recreation pants signify that I can let my hair down and just enjoy hanging out with people I love. Doesn't everybody needs peeps that they can wear their recreation pants in front of without losing face? I wonder if the problem with most politicians and public figures is that they NEVER think it's safe to put on their recreation pants. Who among us can stay "on" 24 x 7? It is impossible. At some point we all need to stop worrying about looking the way we're supposed to look and saying the things we're supposed to say. Sooner or later, we all need to don our recreation pants.

True home is a place filled with people that enjoy my company - even when I'm wearing my recreation pants.

> *"Be grateful for the home you have, knowing that at this moment, all you have is all you need."*
>
> ~*Sarah Ban Breathnach*

Puppy Morning

I am awake before the sun. I want – no I NEED to go to the
bathroom! But puppy is asleep and I can hear it raining outside; do I
really want to wake up puppy and risk a trek outside in the dark
rainy pre-dawn hour? My bladder says YES, so I get up and go to
the bathroom. Puppy is instantly awake and ready to rumble, but
amazingly she settles back down when I return to bed. Thank God
for a crate trained puppy!

The alarm wakes both puppy and me a few hours later. I dress
quickly and take her out for her morning pee. It's still raining and
the sprinklers are running as well. Oh joy. This is the third morning
in a row for the sprinklers.

Apparently we still haven't figure out the sprinkler program.
Mommy dog (that's me) must go out with puppy or puppy won't
do her business – that rule seems to be written in the puppy code! I
am a good dog, so out I go with puppy into the rain. The yard is a
swamp and soon both puppy and I are wet and bedraggled. I stand
in the swampy grass, wondering what the neighbors think of my
"wet dog" in pajamas look!

Finally back inside, mission accomplished. We head upstairs – I
walk, puppy romps right behind me. I feel like breaking into a
chorus of "Me and my Shadow". We wake up the big blonde
"puppy"; my daughter. And she is so thrilled to be awakened at the
crack of dawn – NOT! Why does school starts at the earliest hour for
teenagers? Are we adults cruel hearted, or what?!

I race back downstairs with puppy at my heels. It is time to feed
puppy and 2 very impatient cats. The cats see puppy and hiss their
disdain for this furry interloper. The cats have probably been
plotting puppy's demise all night. Luckily puppy is bigger than
both of them, or puppy would be a chewed up cat toy by now.

Upstairs, downstairs, upstairs again – it is the puppy diet and
exercise plan! Cats fed, check. Puppy fed, check. Daughter fed,
check. Puppy and I head back out into the swamp for puppy's post-

meal pee, check. I sit down – FINALLY – and then my daughter comes in the house to say she has missed the bus somehow; a bus that stops right next to our house. I race upstairs to grab the dog crate for the car, load puppy and daughter up – wait! Mommy dog needs shoes. Finally dressed, I load both puppies into the car and hurry off to school to drop off big blonde puppy.

When we arrive at big puppy's Middle School, it is a ghost town; no cars in the circle, no kids in sight. It is quiet – too quiet. My daughter, puppy and I are the only living souls in the school parking lot. Something is seriously wrong here. Is it Saturday or something?! No, it's definitely Wednesday. So, where is everybody?

"Oh yeah, it's a late start day!" my daughter exclaims. "School starts two hours late today!"... I stare at her in disbelief. What, pray tell, happened to the memo that was supposed to tell mom and dad about THAT?

My daughter laughs hysterically. I laugh with her and turn the car around for home. My daughter has the right idea; what else is there to do except laugh hysterically?

It's been a crazy morning and I am just getting started. It's been a puppy morning.

Follow the Magic

A bit of serendipity…this morning I ended up taking a hike in the mountains. I had an appointment, but the Universe had other plans for me! I was already in town when I found out that my morning appointment was cancelled. What to do with 2 hours? What to do? So many possibilities!

The mountains called out to me, and I found myself driving to meet them. It was a beautiful morning to be outside, sunny and cool with a few inches of day old snow blanketing the mountain. As I began hiking straight uphill in snow, I questioned the wisdom of my decision. But legs and lungs soon adjusted to the climb and the view was enough to keep me going.

Along the way, I relished the silence – what is it about snow on the ground that makes the woods so still? I felt like I was walking in sacred silence. Step by step, I picked my way carefully up and down the snowy slopes. Walking in snow became my morning meditation practice. With each step, my mind cleared and my heart opened wider.

Down in a hollow where I have never hiked before, I met an old Mama pine tree. I stood and listened to her view of the world for a little while.

I leaned against Mama pine's trunk, listening and looking up into her branches, After 5 minutes in her space, I felt like I had been at a meditation retreat for days! And my heart opened even wider.

Thank you, Mama pine, for sharing some of your magic with me.

"Let me bring you songs from the woods,
to make you feel much better than you could know…"

~Jethro Tull

Simple Joys Abound

Day Joy
wool sockslong walk
quiet woodsfriendly dog
sun on frost.

Night Joy
moonless skysoft bed
warm promise
dark quietwinter dreams.

Simple joys abound.

Foment Joy

What the world needs now is
more joy, more humor, more smiles

Get Busy!

When did I decide that adulthood meant being serious and trying to figure it all out?? Blow that idea up! I choose to blow up all the crap I was ever taught about adults being required to get serious and be responsible.

Who decided that mature and serious mean the same thing? No way! Some of the coolest adults I've every met are goofy and irreverent and downright silly. I choose that!

I choose to go for wonder and jump on joy today. Right now, in this moment, I choose irreverence and humor over figuring it all out.

So, what happens when I spend my day focused on joy? Encouraging joy? Searching for joy? Is it possible to get UN-serious at the ripe old age of ... you thought I'd spill my age there, didn't you?! Hah! Let's just say I'm middle aged and leave it at that. I don't know exactly what's possible at my age (and does age even matter??). But I intend to play and explore how far I can take this joy thing.

Want to join me in my frivolity? Or stay serious, if you prefer. But I'm thinking that I'd like some playmates...

Foment   [foh-ment]
verb
to instigate or foster; promote the growth or development of:
to foment trouble; to foment discontent

Dawn Joy Patrol

4am – I wake up to a strange sound… can it be? Yes, it's raining here! Finally. After a brief stint at the window with Dog Goddess Brigit – the smell of wet pine trees is AMAZING (!) – I return to bed and the land of nod.

7am - I prepare to go on Dawn Joy Patrol. My mission? To Hunt down Joy wherever it may be hiding… But first… what do I wear for this special mission?!

7:30am – After a brief descent into angst and indecision, I have chosen an outfit for Joy Patrol! It consists of groovy, yet functional Safari pants (may be rough out there) and a Bedazzled T-shirt. Oh yes, and a silly grin must be part of every Joy uniform.

8am – My ADD gerbil brain flashes on an old photograph I found a few weeks ago of my brother and I reporting for Joy Patrol duty as kids. Today's Joy Patrol mission is happily sidetracked for 10 minutes while I locate the photo in question. I cannot help giggling when I look at it – We were such happy young whippersnappers! Apparently my brother and I knew at a very young age the value of wearing silly glasses and grinning like fiends when you are hunting for joy…

8:15am - Hubby David and I rendezvous at a coffee shop in town for provisions. My Soy Bhakti and Brego are exquisite. Hooray for joyful tastebuds!

However, I find the hip coffee shop crowd to be super serious and unsmiling. When David dares me to whistle, and I comply with a short rendition of "Don't Worry, Be Happy" - people are not amused. The crowd actually appears to be questioning my sanity. Such is the price one pays as a bona fide member of the Joy Patrol. It is a sacrifice I am willing to make…

8:45am – I leave the coffee shop and head out to hunt for joy on a walk with Dog Goddess Brigit. But my search for joy is sidetracked by several streets to nowhere at first. This is a common occurrence when on the road to Joy.

9am – Brigit and I finally arrive at an open space near the north end of town. Despite the rain, Dog Goddess Brigit seems quite happy to report for Joy Patrol this morning.

10am Brigit's full Joy Patrol report is completely illegible – the path was quite muddy; it is hard to type with wet paws. Luckily I am here, ready and willing to translate for the Dog Goddess!

The gist of Brigit's report is as follows:
Yucky part of Dog Joy Patrol in the rain? Drippy nose and ears
Brigit's favorite part? Stinky MUD everywhere!

What is the next stop on my personal Joy Patrol? Who can say? I will happily go wherever Joy has been rumored to be hiding. Stay tuned…

"Joy is the simplest form of gratitude."

~Karl Barth

Joy Flows

Joy spontaneously flows in each of us, as us and from us... when we remember how AMAZING we truly are.

Can I allow myself to BE that space of flowing joy?

What will it take for me to relax into being joy?

What will it take for me to live from that place of flowing joy?

How much joy can I embody and share with the world?

These are the questions I wonder about, that matter to me. Am I truly willing to open to the possibility of more Joy every single day??

"When you do things from your soul,
you feel a river moving in you, a joy."

~Rumi

Morning Joy

*"I arise in the morning torn between a desire to improve the
worldand a desire to enjoy the world.
This makes it hard to plan the day."*

~E.B. White

Why choose one or the other? What if BOTH are possible?

What if I can work with Joy, eat with Joy, move with Joy, live with
Joy AND leave the world a better place?

What if the simple act of going for Joy brings light to the entire
world, to all humanity?

What if the seemingly selfish act of pursuing Joy is the easiest, most
graceful way to change everything?

*EVERYTHING within me that's getting in the way of JOY,
blow it up! Make space for Joy now.*

Vulnerable Joy

What Makes Life Worth Living?

I hope to spend the rest of my life exploring the answer to that question! Researcher Brene Brown claims that human beings live to connect with each other. She spent years interviewing thousands of people and exploring self worth, happiness and the importance of connection.

Brown claims the happiest people share several traits:

> *The **courage** to be imperfect*

> *The **compassion** to be kind to themselves first, and then to others*

> *The ability to create connections as a result of authenticity*

> *The willingness to fully **embrace vulnerability***

I wonder if I can open myself that fully? Can I expose my true self to the world? Will I take the risk even if it means I might get hurt?

> *Will I risk being that vulnerable?*

> *While I am here on this planet, will I choose to keep opening, to keep risking and sharing myself?*

Yes, sometimes I get hurt. Sometimes life is so painful that I want to curl up and never leave the house again. But living life with a closed heart is no life at all. And every single moment of joy I have experienced so far has come from being open.

I choose Open.

I choose Vulnerable.

I choose Joy.

Flowers Whisper

Flowers whisper in the wood, full of hope and possibility.

Flowers sing to me, my heart seems to know their melody.

Flowers smile at me, a holy spirit lights each face.

Flowers bloom pure joy, asking me to join in.

The only sane answer is YES.

Shadow and Joy

*"We are shaped by our thoughts; we become what we think.
When the mind is pure, joy follows like a shadow that never
leaves."*

~Buddha

Joy can be as elusive and slippery as a soap bubble. Yet once, years ago in meditation, I realized that joy and misery lie just a hair's width apart within my mind. I sensed both joy and misery sitting just micrometers apart within my body; and the image was so clear that I startled and came out of my reverie giggling.

I remember that moment in vivid detail even now years later. And I *know* that I can choose whether I will feel joy or misery or something in between in this moment. And I can choose again in the next moment, and the next.

It only takes a tiny shift in my mind to move from misery into joy; a micron of a shift; a slightly altered point of view.

Breathe. And breathe again. Deep, slow breaths that fill both lungs. And drop into my body; feel whatever sensations are present there in my tissues; feel the sensations that joy is hiding behind. Breathe and feel every inch of that body.

Open my heart and allow the joy within me to step out of the shadows and be here now.

Can it really be that simple?

Yes. Yes!

About the Author

Nancy Lankston has been exploring the art and science of healing for over 25 years. She has helped thousands of clients find healing. Nancy loves helping others reconnect with their soul's desires and heal from within. She is also passionate about her efforts to help and heal our beautiful planet.

Nancy currently lives with her family on the edge of the Rocky Mountains. She spends her time writing, hiking, healing and teaching others how to dream and transform their lives.

More of Nancy's poetry and prose can be found online at: *www.nancylankston.com*.

www.ingramcontent.com/pod-product-compliance
Lightning Source LLC
Chambersburg PA
CBHW060941040426
42445CB00011B/953